ETHICS & RELIGIONS

•JOHN RANKIN•ALAN BROWN•PAUL GATESHILL•

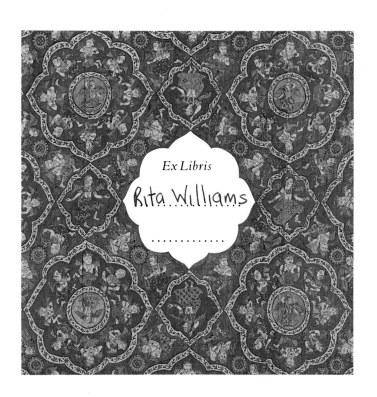

Longman

Contents

The Authors

John Rankin is former Head of Religious Studies at the West Sussex Institute of Higher Education.

Alan Brown is Director of the National Society's RE Centre in London and Schools' Officer (RE) of the Board of Education of the General Synod of the Church of England.

Paul Gateshill, formerly Head of RE at Archbishop Michael Ramsey School in Camberwell, is now Advisory Teacher for Religious Education in the London Borough of Croydon.

We wish to thank the following for their help with specific points in the manuscript:
Ayre Forta
Joy White
Rabbi Douglas Charing
Mathoor Krishnamurti
Mr Rahman (Trustee of Croydon Mosque)
Mr Singh Channa
Mr Chhatwal Singh (Secretary of the Sikh Missionary Society)
Philip Eden (General Secretary of the Buddhist Society)
Indarjit Singh (Editor, *The Sikh Messenger*)
Dr W Owen Cole
Ruth Tayler
Tom Caluori

We are grateful to Margaret Ashby for carrying out school trials and assessing some of the material.
We especially thank Monica Kendall who edited the whole book.

Thanks are due to many others who offered advice and we are glad to acknowledge them also.

Introduction

Human beings are faced with many issues and problems in life. We have decisions to make about how to live together in peace, about how to treat people who have broken the law and about how to prevent our planet from being destroyed. All religions have something to say about these things, but they have never agreed completely about how people should act.

This book takes five important topics and helps you to think about them very carefully, consider the main issues and then look at what a follower of each of six religions might think.

Sometimes issues, such as heart transplants, are so modern that religions do not have any special writings about them. In these cases, we consider what differences belief could make and what some of the religious leaders have said.

Remember that religions are not *only* about making moral decisions, they are about the whole way a person lives – the quality of life and values – and the spiritual strength a person needs.

On pages 6 and 7 you will find a brief introduction to help you understand the way each of six religions looks at the question of right and wrong. Read these initially and then refer to them again as you read and form your own views.

Use the information, ideas and points made in this book as a basis for discussions and for your own further thinking.

Note on the quotations from the Qur'an
For Muslims, the Qur'an is the revealed word of God. This was revealed in Arabic and cannot be translated precisely into any other language. So when passages of the Holy Qur'an are quoted in this book they must be understood as *interpretations* of the Qur'an. Several English versions have been used. When a Muslim source is being quoted, then the version of the Qur'anic verses in it are used.

Six Religions – Where They Stand

Buddhism

Buddhism is a method for achieving **Nirvana**, which is the ultimate goal in Buddhism. 'Goodness' is seen as just part of what you need to reach Nirvana. Buddhists believe in the ideas of **karma** and **rebirth**, which means they believe that this life is not the only one. A person is reborn many times. **Karma** means that what people do now affects the future and the way they will be reborn. Buddhism teaches that the world passes away, and is not real in the end. It is 'impermanent'. While Buddhists take life in the world seriously, they think that we should not be trying so hard to change it.

Christianity

At the heart of Christianity is the idea of *salvation* and a *saviour*. This means that human beings are created by God 'in his own image'. However, human beings are sinful and have not lived up to what they should be, so they are in need of salvation. That salvation is brought by Jesus Christ. Without God's help, people are unable to behave as they ought to, so doing good is very much a matter of God's **grace**. The teaching of Jesus Christ gives certain principles by which his followers are to judge right from wrong. One of his sayings, for example, is, 'Love your neighbour as yourself.'

Hinduism

The name 'Hinduism' applies to a family of religious teachings and practices. The aim of life is to achieve 'liberation' (**moksha**). In the end, liberation is a matter of seeing clearly – of understanding. Good actions are only part of the way in which the aim of liberation is worked for. If you are not 'good' you cannot begin to move along the way. Hindus believe in **samsara**, that is, 'rebirth'. They believe that humans have indestructible souls which enter new bodies when a person dies. This continues until the soul finally achieves liberation and is absorbed into the 'ultimate being' (**Brahman**) and returns no more to earth. The actions in one life will affect the subsequent lives of any soul. This is part of what is understood by the term **karma**.

Islam

Islam teaches that all God's Creation is good, and so wrong behaviour is a matter of human disobedience. The code of law for the Islamic way of life is called the **Shari'ah**. This code comes from two main sources – the **Qur'an** and the **Sunnah**. The Qur'an is the scripture revealed to the Prophet Muhammad, and the Sunnah is the 'way of life' of the Prophet. This is recorded in the **Hadith** (literally, the 'tradition'). Muslims believe that God has provided all the necessary guidance for good conduct and it is up to His creatures to follow that guidance, whether in private or public life.

Judaism

Judaism is the name given to the religion of the Jews. To be Jewish is to belong to a people who continue the ancient nation of Israel. Jews feel that Israel was chosen by God to be his special representative on earth. The task given to Israel was to show God's 'righteousness' or 'holiness' on earth. God's righteousness is expressed in the 'commandments'. These are contained in the **Torah**. Torah and **Talmud** (the collection of the teaching of the rabbis) are the main books of guidance for Jewish people. For Jews, right and wrong actions are first and foremost decided by God's laws.

Sikhism

The **Guru** is the most important single idea in Sikhism. The true Guru is God. He has spoken to humankind through ten historical leaders, each called a Guru. The sacred scriptures eventually replaced human leaders. These scriptures are, too, called guru – **Guru Granth Sahib**. Sikhs also hold the doctrine of **samsara**. That is, our souls are reborn many times until we achieve union with the true Guru. The sign of finding the true Guru is a love and a longing to serve. Sikhism is a religion in which right conduct and truth are closely associated. They believe that there can be no understanding of truth apart from righteous behaviour.

Marriage and Family

1

▼ Introduction

> ▼ **Individually, write down your definition of a 'family'. Begin with 'A family is . . .'. Do this before reading any further. Share what you have written with a neighbour.**

The word 'family' has many meanings. It can mean those people you live with – father, mother, sister, brother. It can also mean a much wider group of people – grandparents, aunts, uncles, nieces, nephews, cousins – almost anyone who is related to you either by birth or by marriage.

> ▼ **Trace your 'family tree' as far back as possible, or draw up an imaginary one, for example:**

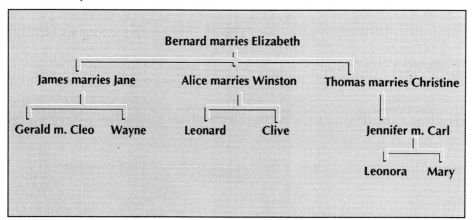

> ▼ **Look at this family tree. James, Alice and Thomas are brothers and sister, but what relation is Gerald to Leonard? Or Wayne to Alice? Or Mary to Bernard?**

A wider family

'Family' can also mean a group of people – even a small group – who agree to share their lives and live together. They are not necessarily related to each other. They 'adopt' and trust each other as if they were related by blood.

The term 'blood relation' usually means a person who is related by direct descent (such as Elizabeth, Alice and Clive in the family tree; Winston is not a blood relation to Elizabeth, he is related 'by marriage' to her). When someone says 'blood is thicker than water' they mean that the fact you are related to someone means more than any friendship.

You may be familiar with the Red Indian term 'blood brother'. The closeness of a relationship and the acceptance of a person as a trusted friend was sealed by the

▼

mingling of blood. It was a serious way of showing their closeness – their strong bond of friendship.

▼   **Is blood thicker than water? Do you think family ties are stronger than friendship? Are they just different? Write down a few ideas.**

A community as a family

Another meaning of 'family' is even broader. It means people who share the same interests, or even *all* people. Some refer to all the people on the earth as 'the human family' because we share so much in common. Some speak of members of their religion as 'family' because they share the same beliefs and worship the same God. In other words, 'family' is also used of people who share an interest, a faith or a common concern.

This family live in Clapham, London. Can you work out how the individuals are related to each other? What type of family is it?

▼ Types of family

As you worked through the previous section you will have realised that we can mean many different things by the word 'family'. In this section we will look at four family types.

Nuclear family

Almost half the people in Britain live in this type of family, though the numbers are decreasing. It means two parents living with one or more children and sharing the same flat or house. They live on their own as a self-contained unit. In Britain the average couple have two children.

One-parent family

One child in eight in Britain is brought up by one parent, usually the mother. The parent may be an unmarried mother who for various reasons does not live with the father of her child. Or the other parent may have died. But usually they are single parents as a result of divorce or separation. In 1987 about 5% of people were single parents. The number had doubled since 1961.

Extended family

This is a larger group of people – grandparents, aunts, uncles, cousins, including people who have come into the family by marriage. This was the typical family unit in the past and is usual in China and India. Today they probably do not live together in one house. They may live far away from each other and only come together at special times – a marriage, a funeral and perhaps for special festival occasions. However, some extended families do live close together, in nearby streets or within walking distance of each other. In some parts of Britain a number of people in a village or a town will be related to each other and form part of an 'extended family'. For some cultures the 'extended' family is the normal family unit.

Community family

This is also known as an 'expanded family'. It is an unusual type of family unit in Britain but it does exist in various forms in other parts of the world. Sometimes a number of people join together to form a community. While any children will 'belong' to their parents, they will be the responsibility of the whole community. The parents may work in the community while the children are cared for by other adults. This type of community is a 'family' with responsibilities to each other, and who act as if they were blood relatives of each other.

▼ **What advantages and disadvantages can you think of for each of these types of family? Discuss them in groups of four or five.**

▼ **List for your own interest your 'extended' family. It may help to think of relatives who have moved away, or who are living in another part of the world.**

The types of family and the role of the family is different in different parts of the world, and has changed over the years. Families mean different things to different people but they are generally believed to be important – to society, to religion and culture. Families involve relationships – between each member of the family and between one family and another.

▼   **In the first exercise on page 8, which of these types of family did you write about?**

These women belong to a kibbutz in Israel. What are they doing? Would you like to live in a community family?

Marriage

ONE of the great upheavals of the age is the changed and still changing status of women in society, leading to changed relationships between the sexes. It is inconceivable that the institution of marriage will not be drastically transformed in the process. There is no evidence that it is dying out. It is no longer fashionable to predict that marriage, in any recognisable form, is about to give way to radically new forms of sexual relationships. Marriage has never been more popular, even if it has never been more risky.

This quotation is from *The Times* newspaper in 1976.

▼ **Read the extract again. Write down two or three words that seem important to you. Compare your list with a neighbour. Have you chosen the same words or not? Try to say why you chose the words you did.**

▼ **The writer says that because the role of women in British society has changed, so marriage will be changed. Why should this happen? Why should the writer think marriage 'has never been more risky'? Write a few sentences giving your view.**

The extract raises important issues which we will return to later. These are: the popularity of marriage; the changing status of women; the changing state of marriage; sexual relationships.

The popularity of marriage

Marriage is more popular in this century than it has ever been. About 90% of the British population will marry during their lifetime, often more than once. In 1987 there were 398,000 weddings in Britain. Throughout the world most people will get married. It is the norm. But marriage has not always been so popular. Before the seventeenth century, in Christian cultures, a celibate life as a monk or nun was more highly valued. During the second half of the nineteenth century, about 40% of all men and women in Britain *never* married.

In Britain the minimum age for marriage is 16 (or 18 when the parents do not have to give their consent). It can be younger in other parts of the world. In Britain people are gradually delaying marriage, though there are still many teenage marriages. In 1987 the average age for men marrying for the first time was 27, for women it was 24. In the Victorian age the bride was usually in her late twenties, the groom in his early thirties. One in five of the marriages today (20%) take place after the couple have lived together.

More and more people are remarrying. In 1987 35% of all marriages were remarriages. More men remarry than women.

Just over 50% of all weddings are religious weddings, the others take place in a register office.

▼ **Why do you think over 50% of weddings each year involve a religious ceremony? (In Britain only about 5–10% out of a population of 57 million attend a place of worship regularly.)**

▼ **Roughly 1,000 couples get married each day. About a third of these will be second or later marriages. Discuss any reasons you can think of why marriage is still popular.**

(left) A Hindu wedding in Wimbledon, London. Look carefully at the picture. Which is the bride and which the bridegroom? Who is the man sitting with them (wearing glasses)? Who is the man sitting on the ground on the left and what is he doing? Describe some of the articles on the floor. What kind of feeling does this ceremony give?

▼ Women and marriage

Married women then

In Victorian Britain the choices open to women were very limited. If they were not able to marry they might have to stay at home and look after their parents, or go into domestic service. Many working-class women worked in factories and workshops, for little money and long hours, and were looked on as cheap labour. Their children were usually looked after by relations. It was almost impossible to be independent.

Married women had few rights over their property or even their children. The husband was totally dominant over them. It was impossible to divorce unless you were very rich, and even then it was more difficult for women to divorce than men.

Victorian families were usually very big. In the 1860s the average number of children was 6.2. As many as 1 in 6 families had ten children or more. So annual pregnancies were common. Infant mortality was high – that is, many children died young. Frequent pregnancies often affected the health of the mother, and some died in childbirth.

> ▼ Why do you think a family consisted of so many children? What kind of lives do you think people lived? If there is an old graveyard near you, look at the nineteenth-century gravestones and work out how old people were when they died.

Married women now

> ▼ Discuss what you think has changed for married women since the mid Victorian period (as described above). Think about 'rights', job opportunities, number of children, divorce (there is more about this on pages 22–3), health. Is there anything else that might have changed the position of married women?

Today there are many more job opportunities for women. Acts of Parliament – such as the Equal Pay Act of 1970 and the Sex Discrimination Act of 1975 – mean that women should have the same job opportunities as men. Women can now be independent.

If they do marry, the husband is no longer dominant by law. Divorce is easier. Some married women do not take their husband's surname, to show that they want to be treated as individuals. Some people believe, however, that there are still inequalities.

The availability of contraception has meant that a couple can delay the time when they start having children, as well as limit the number of children they have. Married women can therefore be employed for a long time before they have children and return to employment afterwards. In 1987 60% of married women took paid employment outside the home. Modern, labour-saving devices and conveniences, such as washing machines and launderettes, supermarkets with 'ready meals' and stores with ready-made clothes have reduced the heavy chores of household work.

On average, however, women get paid less than men. Labour-saving devices may simply have replaced domestic service common in the Victorian period. Women still have the responsibility for caring for the children – in 1987 less than a third of women with children under five worked. The majority of household tasks, such as washing, cleaning and cooking, are still done by women, even when they also have jobs outside the home. In 1987 only 23% of couples shared household cleaning equally; in 72% of couples the women did it. Women's right to work outside the home has not resulted in a sharing of jobs inside the home. Childcare facilities are difficult to find and often expensive.

▼ **How many married women do you know who have a job outside the home? You could start with your own mothers and teachers and design a questionnaire. Find out why they take paid employment. What are the advantages and disadvantages of working outside the home? Does it make any difference if they have children? Discuss the results of your questionnaires.**

▼ **Prepare a TV interview with two married women – one who is in full-time paid employment and the other who is a full-time housewife.**

Although many women with young children want paid employment, there are few childcare facilities and only 3% of employers provide help with childcare. This shows one of the workplace nurseries available. What are the good points for this type of arrangement? Can you think of any disadvantages?

▼ Why do people get married?

▼   **Individually write down if you want to get married eventually or not, and note your reasons.**

There have always been different reasons for getting married. Sometimes it has been to have children to carry on the family line. Sometimes children were needed to provide more labour to work the land.

In Christian cultures, couples who get married today often say they do so because they love each other and want to be together. They may look for sexual and personal fulfilment, for happiness, and support, and to share their lives and interests. Children are no longer the most important reason for marrying and many couples decide not to have children.

▼   **In a small group consider the reasons for getting married. Make a list of six or more reasons and then try to agree the order of importance. Report your findings for a class book or wall display.**

Do you know these people? If you do, do you think they give a good idea of a real family in the TV programme 'Brookside'? Tell those who do not know, about this family

The ideal

Today many people expect a great deal from marriage. They expect to be always in love, to be happy and fulfilled. If it doesn't work they believe they can easily get divorced. Many have an ideal picture of married life – a beautiful, clean, tidy house, with plenty of money, and perfect and dutiful children. Television advertisements normally show the family as a wholesome, happy group, often of two parents and two children. No one loses their temper and meals are carefully prepared!

Is life really like that? Romantic fiction shows a man and a woman falling in love and after many obstacles marrying and living 'happily ever after'. Soap operas use family relationships and arguments as the main part of their story. Weddings and births are often the highlight of the drama.

▼ **Collect advertisements from newspapers, magazines, posters, and make notes of any on television which show a family. What sort of family is it (nuclear, one – parent, extended, etc.)? How many children are there? What type of product is being advertised? You could make a class chart for display, like this:**

Advert	Type of family	Children	Product

▼ **Do you think the examples you have collected reflect real family life? List a number of ways in which they differ.**

▼ **Why do you think advertising uses the family to sell particular products? Make up a TV advertisement using a family and act it out.**

▼ **Discuss the soap operas you know. Do they involve families? What type of families (nuclear, extended etc.)? Do you know families like this in real life? In small groups write a short dramatic scene involving a family that might be part of a soap opera. When you have done this look carefully at how you decided on the content of the scene and which characters played the leading parts.**

Why not just live together?

Many couples do live together, with no intention of marrying. But sometimes when they have children they do decide to marry, though fewer people will than 15 years ago.

Some couples marry because they believe they are fulfilling God's purpose for their lives. They believe marriage is the way God encourages human beings to realise their full potential. Others may want their relationship to be strengthened by rituals and solemn promises – as in the marriage ceremony. Over half of marriages in Britain involve religious ceremonies. Some people who remarry after divorce have their marriages 'blessed' in church. Although a minority of people attend a religious service regularly, they may wish to underline their love for each other in a church, synagogue, or gurdwara, for example.

▼ Sexual relationships and contraception

One of the reasons for marriage is to share a loving, sexual relationship. Most religions, and almost half the population in Britain, believe that sexual relations should take place only within a marriage. Although almost a quarter of couples live together before they marry and many couples live together without ever getting married, a large minority of the population believe that sexual relationships should wait until couples have made a public commitment to each other. Some believe that their sexual relationship will be better and more deeply satisfying if they wait until they are married.

One reason for getting married has been when the woman became pregnant. It is more acceptable in Western society today, however, for a single woman or a couple to have children without being married. In 1989 27% of births in Britain were outside marriage, compared with 4% in the 1900s. But couples often feel they want to give their child a more stable relationship. If the couple are only living together it is quite easy for one partner to walk out; if they are married they have to go to law to end the marriage.

Monogamy

Monogamy (having only one wife or husband) is the law in Britain. **Bigamy** (having two wives or husbands) is a criminal offence and can result in a prison sentence. Some societies allow more than one wife or husband. In parts of Africa the status and wealth of a man is decided by the number of wives he has. This is called **polygamy**. Very few societies allow **polyandry**, in which a woman has more than one husband.

▼ **Divorced people often marry again, so they will marry more than one person, though only one at a time. This is sometimes called 'serial monogamy'. Write down what you think this means.**

Why is monogamy the law in most societies? One reason might be to limit the number of children. A man can father many thousands of children, but if he has only one wife the most he could father would be about thirty.

A short history of contraception

Rough forms of contraceptives (birth control methods) have been used for thousands of years, but they could be dangerous, uncomfortable, never reliable and sometimes forbidden. Some religions still forbid the use of methods other than 'natural' methods. (One 'natural' method is the rhythm method – when women note their fertile and infertile periods and avoid sex during fertile days.) Old methods used objects that acted like the modern cap (inside the vagina) or sheath/condom (used over the penis). At the end of the last century scientific developments led to more reliable condoms and caps. The fight began to make such contraceptives available to all women.

It was a hard and angry struggle. Some people said that if women knew about birth control methods they wouldn't have children any more. They believed it was wrong to tamper with birth or to have sex without the intention of producing children.

A Family Planning clinic in Bangladesh. Can you think of reasons why it is considered important to limit the size of families in this country? What is the main religion practised in Bangladesh?

The Pill

The 'Pill' is the most popular form of contraception. It prevents ovulation (prevents the egg cell from being produced). A woman takes one pill every day for 21 days. Then starts again after a gap of 7 days. It is the most reliable method. There are side effects, however, and not all women can take it. It was introduced into Britain in the 1960s and it changed the approach to contraception dramatically:

1 It was very reliable
2 It was convenient
3 It did not interrupt the sexual act
4 Women were in control of whether they became pregnant or not.

▼ **Do you believe that responsibility for contraception should be shared equally? Write down what you think.**

The Pill had an effect on the sexual attitudes and behaviour of women (and men). Some say it made women freer. Others that it made women feel they ought to 'sleep around' to show how free they were, but that's not what they wanted.

66 I'm 52. The Pill was marvellous for me. I've had two husbands and six lovers. Since taking the Pill I've had no fear of pregnancy.

66 If I hadn't been taking the Pill since I was 14, I probably wouldn't have slept with so many men by now. [18-year-old woman]

▼ Inter-religious and arranged marriages

Arranged marriages

In Britain in past centuries a marriage was not usually between two people who were in love, but between two families. For wealthy and land-owning families, in particular, marriage was to do with property, money, and continuing the family line. Marriages were therefore 'arranged'. This view of marriage can still be seen today when the newspapers debate who would be a suitable groom or bride for a member of the royal family.

In other countries, and in Britain among some groups such as Muslims, Hindus and Sikhs, marriages are still arranged or 'assisted'. This will happen for different reasons in the different religious and cultural groups. Sometimes there are only a small number of suitable partners, and families need to be introduced to each other. Judaism no longer supports arranged marriages, but there are marriage agencies that specialise in bringing Jewish people together. Arranged marriages are not forced marriages. This is clearly shown in a letter to a newspaper which expresses one Muslim point of view:

Dear Sir,

As far as Islam is concerned, it does not recognise forced marriages. According to Islamic laws relating to matrimony, both the bride and groom have to consent to a marriage before it can be solemnised. This consent has to be expressed, not once but thrice, in the presence of adult witnesses before the service can proceed.

All that 'arranged marriage' means is that the bride and groom, instead of yielding to their infatuations, put their faith in the loving care and mature judgement of their respective seniors. Even so, they are at liberty to withhold consent if they disagree with the choice made by their seniors – and thus block the solemnisation of the marriage.

Parents who arrange marriages believe that they know their children better than anyone and therefore know what sort of person their children will be happiest with. Love is important, but they believe it should grow after marriage, not before. It is important to realise that arranged marriages are not necessarily cruel or heartless. They are part of a long tradition, sometimes used to seal great friendships between families. The parents do their best to ensure a happy life for their children.

▼   **What are the advantages of an arranged marriage?**
    Are there disadvantages?
    Do you think parents might be a better judge of who is a good partner than the young people themselves?
    Discuss these questions with a friend or in a small group.

Inter-religious marriages

Sometimes men and women from different faiths marry. For many people their religion is not important, but for some people and religious communities it is very important, and they are very worried if their young people marry outside the religion. They wonder whether the children will be brought up in the father's or mother's religion. Will one of the partner's abandon their religion or even be converted to their partner's faith? In religions where marriages are usually arranged, to go against parental wishes can cause pain and family upset.

The couple may marry in a register office and will be married as far as the State is concerned, but they will not be married as far as their religion is concerned.

▼   **It might be very difficult for a Jew and a Christian to marry in a church or synagogue. Why? What religious claims would be made upon both persons that would make it difficult for one or the other? Try to ask a rabbi or a Christian minister about this. Are there any statements in the Jewish or Christian marriage ceremonies which would make either of them uncomfortable? Make a note of these.**

A Muslim woman is not allowed to marry anyone other than a Muslim, but a Muslim man may marry a Jewish or Christian woman:

66   And the chaste from among the believing women and the chaste from among those who have been given the Book before you are lawful for you.[Qur'an 5:5] For some Jews, inter-marriage is also forbidden:

66   You must not intermarry with them, neither giving your daughters to their sons nor taking their daughters for your sons.   [Deuteronomy 7:3]

Some Reform rabbis, however, will marry a Jew to a non-Jew (Gentile) though the Gentile partner may promise that any children will be raised as Jews. Orthodox Jews, however, would be unhappy if their son or daughter were to marry even a Reform Jew, that is a Jew from a non-Orthodox branch of Judaism.

Among Christians, some Roman Catholics and Protestants would not wish their children to marry outside their particular denomination of Christianity.

▼   **In groups discuss:**
    Why might some Christians not wish their children to marry Christians from another denomination? Would it matter so long as they were Christian?
    What are some of the problems which married people of different faiths might have to deal with?

▼ Divorce

 We see . . . how few matrimonies there be without chidings, brawlings, tauntings, repentings, bitter cursings and fightings.

This was written in 1571 during the reign of Elizabeth I. It is common to have rows in marriage, but only recently has it been acceptable for married people in Britain to divorce.

Between 1697 and 1855 in England and Wales there were only 317 divorces. We know, because at that time every divorce had to take place by an Act of Parliament. Only the very wealthy could afford them.

Divorce courts were set up in 1857, and made available to everyone, but it was still very expensive. It was also easier for a man to get a divorce than a woman, and there were many people (especially religious people) who were strongly against couples divorcing.

The Divorce Reform Act

In 1969 the divorce laws were changed and made divorce easier and cheaper. This Act came into effect in 1971 and resulted in a huge increase in the number of divorces – as you can see in the table below. Most decrees were granted to women. Most divorces take place after a couple have been married between five and nine years.

A couple could now get a divorce if one partner had behaved 'unreasonably'. This might include physical violence or verbal abuse – simply unreasonable behaviour. In 1987 over half the decrees granted to wives were for this reason. Most men were granted divorce for their wives' adultery.

If a couple separated they could be divorced after two years if both agreed. If one partner did not agree then they could be divorced after five years of living apart. In 1984 the Matrimonial and Family Proceedings Act made it possible to get a divorce after one year of marriage and also enabled divorced men to reduce the financial support they had to give to their former wives.

		Marriages		Divorces	
1961	346,700	♥♥♥♥♥♥♥♥♥♥♥♥♥♥♥♥♥♥♥♥♥♥♥♥♥♥♥♥♥♥♥♥		25,400	♡♡♡
1966	384,500	♥♥♥♥♥♥♥♥♥♥♥♥♥♥♥♥♥♥♥♥♥♥♥♥♥♥♥♥♥♥♥♥		39,100	♡♡♡♡
1971	404,700	♥♥♥♥♥♥♥♥♥♥♥♥♥♥♥♥♥♥♥♥♥♥♥♥♥♥♥♥♥♥♥♥		74,400	♡♡♡♡♡♡♡♡
1975	380,600	♥♥♥♥♥♥♥♥♥♥♥♥♥♥♥♥♥♥♥♥♥♥♥♥♥♥♥♥♥♥♥♥		120,500	♡♡♡♡♡♡♡♡♡♡♡♡
1980	370,000	♥♥♥♥♥♥♥♥♥♥♥♥♥♥♥♥♥♥♥♥♥♥♥♥♥♥♥♥♥♥♥♥		148,300	♡♡♡♡♡♡♡♡♡♡♡♡♡♡♡
1983	344,300	♥♥♥♥♥♥♥♥♥♥♥♥♥♥♥♥♥♥♥♥♥♥♥♥♥♥♥♥♥♥		147,500	♡♡♡♡♡♡♡♡♡♡♡♡♡♡♡
1985	346,400	♥♥♥♥♥♥♥♥♥♥♥♥♥♥♥♥♥♥♥♥♥♥♥♥♥♥♥♥♥♥♥♥		160,300	♡♡♡♡♡♡♡♡♡♡♡♡♡♡♡♡
1987	352,000	♥♥♥♥♥♥♥♥♥♥♥♥♥♥♥♥♥♥♥♥♥♥♥♥♥♥♥♥♥♥♥♥		151,000	♡♡♡♡♡♡♡♡♡♡♡♡♡♡♡

▼　The table on page 22 shows the figures for England and Wales. Discuss what it tells you. For example, are the number of divorces continuing to increase? What about marriages? How many marriages will fail, according to this table?

The figures in the table show the number of all marriages and divorces – *not* the number of *first* marriages or *first* divorces. A large proportion of divorced people eventually remarry – though far more men than women. In 1975, of the 380,600 marriages, nearly one-third involved the remarriage of one or both partners. Second marriages break up even faster than first ones. So redivorce is more common. A recent survey showed that marriage is more popular in Britain (and Portugal) than anywhere else in Western Europe, but has the second highest divorce rate (after Denmark).

▼　If more than 1 in 3 marriages will fail, discuss why you think so many people marry again.

The effect on people's lives

In the 1975 figures, the 120,500 couples who were divorced had 202,470 children (of whom 145,000 – over half – were under 16). So the total number of people directly affected by divorce in 1975 was over 440,000 – the population of a large city. Many of these divorced couples will develop new relationships and have children with new partners. Many of the divorced women will become single parents. Many men will have two families to support.

Although divorce is easier to arrange, it can (and often does) cause much suffering.

▼　Think about the possible effects of divorce on the various people involved – the man, the woman, the children. Share your ideas with another person.

Why do people divorce?

There are a number of reasons. A few are mentioned above and on previous pages – such as, adultery, cruelty or 'unreasonable' behaviour. Couples sometimes marry too young and grow away from each other, love dies and there is nothing else to keep them together. Couples expect too much from a marriage and are disappointed. Because divorce is easy, couples don't work as hard as they could at making their marriage work.

▼　What you would include under 'unreasonable behaviour'? Make a list.

▼　Do you think divorce should be easy or difficult to obtain?
Some people say that it is now too easy – a partnership is bound to be difficult at times and easier divorce laws may mean that couples do not work as hard as they could at making their relationship work. What is your opinion? Write a page explaining your views.

▼　What matters would need to be sorted out when a couple divorce? Try to make a full list in a group of four or five.

Marriage and Family: Religions

 Buddhism

Religious life and family life

The goal of a Buddhist is Nirvana. Disciples gathered around the Buddha and formed a monastic order. For some Buddhists, to be a monk or a nun is a superior way of life to any other because they believe it will help them reach Nirvana.

Most Buddhists, however, do marry and have families. They support the monks and perhaps hope that in the next life they will be monks. The Buddha did not lay down any marriage ritual, but he did talk about what a marriage should be and about the duties of husbands and wives.

Customs vary throughout the Buddhist world. In some countries it is not a religious occasion, but a monk may be invited to recite part of the scriptures at the wedding, or the couple may go to a monastery for a blessing.

Some sects in Buddhism, in China or Japan for example, have different views on marriage. Many of the religious leaders are married and marriage services have been developed. In the marriage ceremony in the Pure Land sect the priest says:

A Buddhist wedding ceremony in a monastery in Nepal. The couple wear 'kartags' – white scarves of cotton around their necks – as symbols of blessing. The lama (the word for a monk in this branch of Buddhism) can be seen sitting on the throne in the background

RELIGIONS

> May the wisdom of the Blessed One shine within our hearts, so that the mists of error and the foolish vanity of self may be dispelled. . . . remember that it is the duty of the husband to support and cherish his wife, to be faithful to her, to comfort her in sickness and sorrow, and to assist in bringing up the children. It is the duty of the wife to love and help her husband, to be patient and gentle in her manner, and to be faithful to him always.

The Buddha told one married couple:

> If, householders, both wife and husband hope to be in one another's sight so long as this life lasts and in the future life as well, they should have the same faith, the same virtue, the same generosity, the same wisdom; then they will be in one another's sight so long as this life lasts and in the future life as well.

▼ **Do you agree or disagree with the teaching that the couple should be of the same faith? Would it be important to you? Write down your opinion to share with others in the class.**

Relations between husband and wife

The relationship is called 'sadara-Brahmacariya' – meaning 'sacred family life'. Men and women are seen as equal, but they have different roles.

> Towards my wife I undertake to – love and respect her, be kind and considerate, be faithful, delegate domestic management, provide gifts to please her.
[Sigalovada Sutta]

> Towards my husband I undertake to – perform my household duties efficiently, be hospitable to my in–laws and friends of my husband, be faithful, protect and invest our earnings, discharge my responsibilities lovingly and conscientiously.
[Sigalovada Sutta]

The faithfulness of husband and wife is very important. The Buddha taught:

> Let the wise man avoid an unchaste life, as he would a burning heap of coals; if he cannot live a life of chastity he should not transgress with another man's wife.

▼ **Look again at the quotations above. Discuss if you think the balance of what is asked of husband and wife is just. What do they tell you about the society at the time they were written?**

▼ **Do you think it is helpful to have your duties clearly set out so you know what is expected of you? Would you change any of the duties above? Produce your own version of a husband's and wife's duties.**

Contraception and divorce

Buddhists will normally follow the practice of the society in which they live, though they would do nothing which might break the Buddhist way of life. These are summed up in the five basic rules or 'precepts' (see page 66). The first precept is: 'To keep from harming others'. Some forms of contraception would therefore be acceptable, as would divorce if the society allowed it.

RELIGIONS

† Christianity

Religious life and family life

 While Jesus was still speaking to the people, behold, his mother and his brothers stood outside, asking to speak to him. But he replied to the man who told him, 'Who is my mother, and who are my brothers?' And stretching out his hand towards his disciples, he said, 'Here are my mother and my brothers. For whoever does the will of my Father in heaven is my brother, and sister, and mother.'

[Matthew 12:46–50]

▼ **Is Jesus rejecting his mother and brothers? In groups discuss what you think he meant.**

Christianity values marriage and family life highly, but at times it has valued celibacy more (that is, being unmarried and having no sexual relations). As far as we know, Jesus was celibate.

Peter and some other of Jesus' disciples were married, but we know that Paul was celibate and thought it better than marriage. But he realised it was not for everyone. In one of his letters he says:

 It is well for a man not to touch a woman. But because of the temptation to immorality, each man should have his own wife and each woman her own husband . . . For the wife does not rule over her own body, but the husband does; likewise the husband does not rule over his own body, but the wife does. . . . I wish that all were as I myself am. But each has his own special gift from God . . . To the married I give charge, not I but the Lord, that the wife should not separate from her husband (but if she does, let her remain single or else be reconciled to her husband) – and that the husband should not divorce his wife.

[1 Corinthians 7:1–2, 4, 7, 10–11]

▼ **What advantages or disadvantages would an unmarried person have if they wished to devote their lives to God? Write a few sentences explaining your answers.**

The Roman Catholic Church believes that the family is the basic cell of human society. They and some other Christians think of marriage as a sacrament – that is, a religious action which channels a blessing from God. The Church of England service describes marriage in this way:

 The Scriptures teach us that marriage is a gift of God in creation and a means of his grace, a holy mystery in which man and woman become one flesh.

Relations between husband and wife

 Wives, be subject to your husbands, as to the Lord. For the husband is the head of the wife as Christ is the head of the church . . . As the church is subject to Christ, so let wives also be subject in everything to their husbands. Husbands, love your wives . . .

[Ephesians 5:22–5]

A wedding in a Greek Orthodox church in London. The priest puts garlands on the heads of the bride and bridegroom. Find out what this 'crowning' means. Notice that the men present are standing together. The women are also standing together out of camera shot on the right. Do you know of any other place of worship where men and women are generally separate? What else do you notice in the picture?

▼ **The passage from Ephesians was probably written by Paul. Is what the writer says suitable for today? Should religious views change as society changes? Make a short summary of the opinions of your group.**

Most Christian couples will make vows during the service. They are the same for both the man and woman. In the Roman Catholic service the priest says:

66 May her husband put his trust in her
and recognise that she is his equal
and the heir with him to the life of grace.

In the Church of England service the priest asks if they will love, comfort, honour and protect each other. They also promise to be faithful to each other whatever happens:

RELIGIONS

 Marriage is given, that husband and wife may comfort and help each other, living faithfully together in need and in plenty, in sorrow and in joy.

Children are considered an important part of marriage.

 [Marriage] is given, that they may have children and be blessed in caring for them and bringing them up in accordance with God's will . . .

The Roman Catholic Church states:

 By its very nature the institution of marriage and married love is ordered to be the procreation and education of the offspring and it is in them that it finds its crowning glory ... The intimate union of marriage, as a mutual giving of two persons, and the good of the children, demand total fidelity from the spouses and require an unbreakable unity between them.

▼ **Look again at what the above quotations say marriage is for. List what purposes *you* think marriage is for.**

Contraception

We have already seen that marriage is for the 'procreation and education' of children. However, most Churches allow contraception and leave decisions about the method to the individual.

But the Roman Catholic Church believes that:

 Life must be protected with the utmost care from the moment of conception . . . In all questions of birth regulation the sons of the Church, faithful to these principles, are forbidden to use methods disapproved of by the teaching authority of the Church in its interpretation of the divine law.

The teaching of the Roman Catholic Church is against all artificial methods of birth control, since it believes that artificial methods stop the creative function of intercourse. A family can still be planned, however, if sexual intercourse only takes place on days when the egg is least likely to be fertilised. The positive elements of this method – the rhythm method (see page 18) – is that it is natural, and that it involves *both* partners in deciding when to have sexual relations.

Divorce

 The question was put to him: 'Is it lawful for a man to divorce his wife?' This was to test him. He asked in return, 'What did Moses command you?' They answered, 'Moses permitted a man to divorce his wife by note of dismissal.' Jesus said to them, 'It was because you were so unteachable that he made this rule for you; but in the beginning, at the creation, God made them male and female. For this reason a man shall leave his father and mother, and be made one with his wife; and the two shall become one flesh. It follows that they are no longer two individuals: they are one flesh. What God has joined together, man must not separate.' When they were indoors again the disciples questioned him about this matter; he said to them, 'Whoever divorces his wife and marries another commits adultery against her: so too, if she divorces her husband and marries another, she commits adultery.'

[Mark 10:2–12]

A man who divorces his wife must give her a note of dismissal. But what I tell you is this: If a man divorces his wife for any cause other than unchastity he involves her in adultery; and anyone who marries a divorced woman commits adultery.

[Matthew 5:31–2]

These passages from the Gospels suggest that marriage is for life. The second passage, however, implies that divorce might be possible on the grounds of adultery.

Christian Churches have different views about divorce, though it is seen as something to be regretted.

The Orthodox Churches believe that while divorce should be avoided it should not mean that a life of celibacy be forced upon an innocent partner. So, given some safeguards, it allows remarriage. The same position is true for the Methodist and the United Reformed Churches, though no minister may be forced to conduct a marriage ceremony against their will.

The issue of divorced people remarrying is much discussed in the Church of England. The law of the land does allow a clergyman to marry a divorced couple, but this goes against the regulations of the Church. These state that a divorced person cannot be married in church if the previous partner is alive. More usual is for a divorced couple to marry in a register office and then have a 'service of prayer and dedication' in a church. But not all clergymen would agree to it.

The Roman Catholic Church does not recognise divorce. Therefore there can be no remarriage. Some Roman Catholics have had their marriages declared 'null'. This means that it was not a proper marriage in the first place. There can be various reasons:

1 the marriage was not consummated sexually
2 the couple were so young when married they did not understand what they were undertaking
3 if either partner was suffering from a nervous problem and was therefore unaware of what was happening.

An annulment nearly always takes a long time and can be expensive.

 Any remarriage is held to be contrary to Christian morality. Christians who infringe [break] the law are not excommunicated [expelled from the Church] but are excluded from the sacramental life of the Church.

▼   **Discuss these questions in small groups:**
    If there is to be a divorce, what should be acceptable grounds (reasons)?
    Is the view of the Roman Catholic Church the most correct? If marriage is for life, shouldn't it mean life?
    Do you think the other Churches have compromised with society? Why do you think they have altered their views?
    Do you think people would prefer to get married knowing they could not divorce? If people know they can divorce do you think they might not try hard enough to make the marriage work?

▼   **Arrange a class debate on 'The Christian View of Divorce'.**

R E L I G I O N S

 **Hinduism**

Religious life and family life

Hinduism divides life into four stages or ashramas:

1 When one learns – pupil
2 Married life – householder
3 Retirement from society – forest-dweller
4 Renunciation of the world – homeless, religious mendicant

Few Hindus follow these stages in real life but they are seen as the ideal way of life, each one following on from the last. The second stage is for earning a living, marriage, having children and educating them. It is important for society. It is also important to have children, especially boys, in order to go on to the next two stages and avoid rebirth. Children continue the family line and light the parents' funeral pyre.

Marriages are arranged by the parents and are a social contract between families. An astrologer-priest ensures that the couple are suited to each other and that they are married on a favourable day. The following is a hymn often used in the marriage ceremony:

 May we be happy with offspring, may we be blessed with *dharma* [e.g. moral right-
eousness].
Bless us, protect us, and help us to respect elders and follow a righteous path for
ever.
Give us strength to follow the path of the 'householder', the man to become a
gentleman and woman to be an ideal wife.
May (our) children behave in the same way.

Relations between husband and wife

At the marriage service the bride's father says:

 She is given as a collaborator in the performance of duties which a householder
ought to perform. She is to inspire and stimulate and she is to lead you on in the
path of dharma.

At the ceremony the bridgroom vows to be faithful, loyal, to share with and care for his wife. The bride has only one vow – that of obedience to her husband.

 Where the women are respected, there lives God. If the wife is obedient to the
husband, and the husband loves his wife; if the children obey the parents, and the
guests are entertained; if the family duty is performed and gifts are given to the
needy, then there is Heaven and nowhere else.

A woman's place is seen as in the home. After marriage she takes on the responsibility of managing the home. She will teach the children and be responsible for their religious upbringing. It is the woman who conducts worship in the home.

 Go to your husband's home and take charge of it. Occupy the main position and
carry out all the activities connected with the home. Here may you have children
and increase your happiness.

Elaborate preparations are made for a Hindu wedding. The custom of preparing the bride is common in most religions. What can you see being done here? Compare this with any other customs you know. Why do you think there is a special preparation?

RELIGIONS

RELIGIONS

In Hinduism the idea of the Mother Goddess has a place of great importance. This shows the high place women, and particularly the mother, have in Hinduism.

 Let your mother be a god to you. Let your father be a god to you.

 The God [Agri] is the wife at home, hastening to help us all.

 Where women are worshipped there the gods love to dwell.

It is partly because of this high esteem that the role of the man in the house can seem overprotective.

 The father protects the woman in childhood, the husband protects her in youth, the children protect her in old age, a woman should never be independent.

▼ **Read the extracts again carefully. Write down why you think the bride is expected to lead the groom 'in the path of dharma'.**

▼ **In many books on Hinduism the importance of the Mother Goddess is explained. In small groups gather as much information as possible about the Mother Goddess. How does your information relate to the role and status of the wife in a Hindu marriage?**

Polygamy

The Hindu scriptures allow polygamy in principle as long as the husband can keep all his wives happy. It does not allow polyandry (women having more than one husband) and forbids a widow from remarrying. In the past only a few wealthy men had more than one wife, however, and it was usually disapproved of unless the first wife was unable to have (especially male) children. The ideal was monogamy. Indian law now forbids polygamy and allows remarriage.

Contraception and divorce

Until recently Hindus would have as many children as they could. But today, especially because of the threat of overpopulation in India, contraception is permitted, even encouraged.

Orthodox Hindus believe the marriage vows to be for life. The Scriptures do not allow divorce. However, Indian law now allows divorce, although it is quite rare, and of course divorce under British law is legal.

▼ **Write a short paragraph outlining the responsibilities of a new Hindu bride.**

 # Islam

Religious life and family life

 And He it is Who has created man from the water, and He has made for him blood-relationship and marriage-relationship. [Qur'an 25:54]

Family life is very important in Islam. Marriage is the way in which Islamic society is bound together – it is the basis of Islamic society. The Prophet Muhammad himself was married. Islamic teachings encourage Muslims to marry and live together in harmony and love, to have children and bring them up as good believing Muslims. A well-known Hadith (a collection of sayings, in this case traced back to the Prophet Muhammad) says:

 No institution in Islam finds more favour with God than marriage. [1:175]

Marriages are normally arranged by the families, with the agreement of the couple. Marriage is a social contract but a sacred one as well. At least two adult Muslims should be present at the marriage to witness the exchange of vows. Both partners sign a written contract and the bride usually receives a dowry (mahr) from the bridegroom (this can be property, jewellery and money). In Britain the couple must also marry in a register office.

The Prophet Muhammad often recited one of the following on the occasion of a marriage:

 O you who believe, fear Allah and let every soul look to what it sends forth for the morrow. [Qur'an 59:18]

 A woman is taken in marriage for three reasons; for her beauty, for family connections or the lure of wealth. Choose the one with faith and you will have success. [Hadith 4:23–5]

This Muslim family at prayer in Winchester are celebrating the festival of Eid

RELIGIONS

Relations between husband and wife

 And one of His signs is that He created mates for you from yourselves that you may find quiet of mind in them and He put between you love and compassion.

[Qur'an 30:21]

The Prophet made clear the relationship between women and men in marriage in his farewell speech:

 People, your wives have certain rights over you and you have certain rights over them. Treat them well and be kind to them, for they are your partners and committed helpers.

Wives and mothers have important positions in Islam. Women have different roles from men. Each have their duties and rights. Some women believe they are better off in a Muslim society, for their rights are protected by Islamic law and they are respected as women. They accept the different roles of men and women, for they see the two sexes as having different, but equally important, responsibilities.

Polygamy

Mostly marriage in Islam is one man with one woman (monogamy). However, the Qur'an does allow a man to marry up to four wives (polygamy). There are conditions: a man must be just to each of them. Today it is discouraged by civil law.

 . . . Marry such women as seem good to you, two and three and four; but if you fear that you will not do justice between them, then only one . . .   [Qur'an 4:3]

 You will not be able to deal justly between your wives, however much you might wish. Do not turn completely aside so that you leave the other in suspense; if you keep proper conduct and do your duty, Allah is always forgiving and merciful.

[Qur'an 4:129]

The Prophet said:

 A man who marries two women and then does not deal justly with them will be resurrected with half his faculties paralysed.

Contraception

Islamic opinion is not at one on this topic. In deciding what is acceptable or not there is little that can be quoted from texts. Decisions are made on inference (that is, taking a similar argument on another topic and drawing a parallel conclusion) and individual discretion. In 1937 Sheikh 'Abdul-Majid Salim, Grand Mufti of Egypt said:

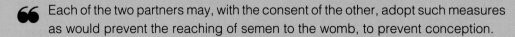 Each of the two partners may, with the consent of the other, adopt such measures as would prevent the reaching of semen to the womb, to prevent conception.

In 1953 a committee of Al-Azhar University, Cairo, wrote:

 The use of drugs to prevent pregnancy temporarily is not forbidden . . . particularly if concern is felt for the woman's life or health as a result of too frequent pregnancies.

However, it is strictly forbidden to take a drug to prevent pregnancy permanently.

Two passages often quoted from the Qur'an when Muslims consider this matter are:

> God wishes you ease and wishes not your discomfort. [2:185]

> He has elected you, and has not laid on you any hardship in religion. [22:78]

In 1959 Sheikh Mahmud Shaltut advised that:

> Women who are frequently pregnant or who have a communicable disease, are too weak 'in their nerves' to take responsibility . . . A certain degree of birth control, if carried out on an individual basis only, is a remedial measure recommended to ward off certain harm and to ensure sound, healthy offspring. Birth control in this sense does not violate the laws of nature – nor is it prohibited in Islam.

Finally, in the Hadith there is a story:

> Jabir b'Abdullah reported that a man came to the Prophet and asked him about sexual intercourse with a slave-girl of his whom he did not want to get pregnant. The Prophet's answer was: 'Practise coitus interruptus [withdrawal method] with her if you wish. What is pre-ordained for her will certainly befall her.
> [Hadith 1:269; 2:92; 5:105]

Divorce

Divorce is permitted in Islam but the Prophet said that of all the things that were permitted, divorce is the most obnoxious (or hateful). Before a divorce can be granted at least three attempts must be made by three different people to reconcile the couple.

> And if a woman fears ill usage or desertion on the part of her husband, there is no blame on them if they effect a reconciliation between themselves, and reconciliation is better . . . And if they separate, Allah will render them both free from want out of His abundance. [Qur'an 4:128–30]

If the man wishes to divorce his wife he must repeat 'I divorce you' in front of witnesses three times, with a month in between each time. He must also pay his ex-wife the rest of the dowry which was reserved in case of divorce.

A woman has the right to divorce her husband but must justify it in a Muslim court. In Britain the husband and wife must also be legally divorced in a British court of law.

Divorced women must not remarry for three months in case they are pregnant. After divorce marriage is allowed for both parties.

▼ **What reasons can you give as to why marriage is so important in Islam? Discuss this in a group and write down your conclusions.**

▼ **Discuss the following: 'Islam represents a well-balanced view of marriage. Parents are careful to ensure a good marriage for their children, children are raised as good Muslims, husbands and wives respect each other.' Why do you think some Muslims are concerned about the effect of non-Muslim society on their children?**

RELIGIONS

R E L I G I O N S

✡ Judaism

Religious life and family life

 . . . male and female he created them. God blessed them and said to them, 'Be fruitful and increase, fill the earth and subdue it.' [Genesis 1:27–8]

 Then the Lord God said, 'It is not good for the man to be alone. I will provide a partner for him.' So God formed out of the ground all the wild animals and all the birds of heaven. . . . but for the man himself no partner had yet been found. And so the Lord God put the man into a trance, and while he slept, he took one of his ribs and closed the flesh over the place. The Lord God then built up the rib, which he had taken out of the man, into a woman. He brought her to the man, and the man said:

> 'Now this, at last-
> bone from my bones,
> flesh from my flesh –
> this shalt be called woman,
> for from man was this taken.'

That is why a man leaves his father and mother and is united to his wife, and the two become one flesh. [Genesis 2:18–24]

 Honour your father and your mother. [Exodus 20:12/Deuteronomy 5:16]

The role of the family in Judaism is very important. This is why many Jews do not want their children to marry non-Jews. Judaism stresses harmony and unity in family relationships. The family protects its members and helps preserve the Jewish faith. The home is the centre of Jewish religious life.

One sign of the importance of the family can be seen in the 'mezuzah'. This is a small box, perhaps 7 cm by 2 cm, which is placed on the side of the door in a Jewish home. It contains two paragraphs in Hebrew from the Torah (the Books of Moses – the first five books of the Bible), which begin:

 Hear, O Israel, the Lord is our God, one Lord, and you must love the Lord your God with all your heart and soul and strength. And these commandments which I give you this day are to be kept in your heart; you shall repeat them to your sons, and speak of them indoors and out of doors, when you lie down and when you rise. [Deuteronomy 6:4–7]

In other words, the family unit is the place where children are taught. But more than that: the teaching of the children and the relationships in the family are intertwined with the Jew's relationship with God.

This is a passage from the marriage contract in the Reform congregation of Jews, which shows the closeness of the Jewish family:

 Accordingly they both entered into this covenant of love and companionship of peace and friendship to create a Jewish home to the glory of the Holy One, blessed be He, who makes His people Israel holy through the covenant of marriage.

▼ Why do you think Jews emphasise the importance of the family so much? Write down your views.

▼ Psalms 84 and 100 are often read at Jewish weddings. Look them up in a Bible. Discuss why you think these two in particular are so frequently used.

A Jewish family observes the feast of Sukkot (Tabernacles). Look up Leviticus 23:39–43. This feast reminds the Jews of the days when they were a nomadic people

RELIGIONS

RELIGIONS

Relations between husband and wife

 Every man needs a woman and every woman a man, and both of them need the divine presence. [Rabbinic saying]

 When a man is newly married, he shall not be liable for military service or any other public duty. He shall remain at home exempt from service for one year and enjoy the wife he has taken. [Deuteronomy 24:5]

Jewish wives and mothers have always been highly esteemed in Judaism. They have an important role in the home and in teaching their children. Every Friday evening at the start of Sabbath some Jews read out the last chapter of Proverbs:

 Who can find a capable wife?
Her worth is far beyond coral.
Her husband's whole trust is in her,
and children are not lacking.
She repays him with good, not evil,
all her life long . . .
She is clothed in dignity and power
and can afford to laugh at tomorrow.
When she opens her mouth, it is to speak wisely,
and loyalty is the theme of her teaching. [Proverbs 31:10–12, 25–6]

▼ **Read the rest of this chapter in Proverbs. What does it say are the qualities of an ideal Jewish wife?**

Polygamy

Some men in Jewish history have had more than one wife at a time – Abraham, Isaac, King David and King Solomon. The Torah permits polygamy but not polyandry (that is, a woman having more than one husband at a time). In the eleventh century CE, Rabbenu (Rabbi) Gersham banned polygamy under Jewish law. But 'Levirate marriage' is accepted:

 When brothers live together and one of them dies without leaving a son, his widow shall not marry outside the family. Her husband's brother shall have intercourse with her; he shall take her in marriage and do his duty by her as her husband's brother. The first son she bears shall perpetuate the dead brother's name so that it may not be blotted out from Israel. [Deuteronomy 25:5–6]

Polygamy has not happened in Judaism since about the 2nd–3rd centuries CE. In 1950 a conference of rabbis met in Israel and renewed the ban on polygamy instituted by Rabbenu Gersham. Monogamy is binding on all Jews.

Contraception

Orthodox Jews believe it is good to have many children. This is because of God's command to procreate, and in order to preserve the Jewish faith. Contraception therefore is only acceptable if the mother's health is at risk.

There is a Jewish law that semen should not be 'wasted' or 'destroyed'. The use of a condom by the man is therefore forbidden unless pregnancy will cause injury or death to the wife.

Generally, Jewish law also disapproves of vasectomy because it prevents the man fulfilling his duty to 'be fruitful and increase'. (Vasectomy is an operation carried out on men which stops the sperm mixing with the semen and entering the woman during intercourse. It makes a man sterile.) However, since some vasectomies can nowadays be reversed, in recent years some rabbis have permitted the operation.

Some rabbis object to women using contraceptive devices which interfere with the passage of the semen. Generally today almost all rabbinic authorities allow the woman to use contraceptive devices if her mental or physical health is a matter of concern. The use of the Pill is permitted after the couple have given birth to a boy and a girl.

▼ **Share your views in a group regarding the rabbinic judgements on contraception. Is too much responsibility placed on one partner? In discussion, can you see the way in which the rabbis have made the text relevant today?**

Divorce

66 Over him who divorces the wife of his youth, even the altar of God sheds tears.

Divorce is greatly regretted in Judaism, as the above quotation shows. However, Judaism believes that if a husband and wife cannot live together then divorce is sometimes the best solution, even when there are children involved. But it is quite rare.

66 When a man has married a wife, but she does not win his favour because he finds something shameful in her, and he writes her a note of divorce, gives it to her and dismisses her. . . . [Deuteronomy 24:1]

As marriage is sealed with a contract, so a note of divorce (called a 'get') is needed. (In Britain a civil divorce would have to be obtained first.) This document is given to the wife by the husband. Here is an extract:

66 Thus I do set you free, release you, and put you aside, in order that you may have permission and authority over yourself to go and marry any man you may desire. No person may hinder you from this day onward, and you are permitted to every man. This shall be for you from me a bill of dismissal, a letter of release, and a document of freedom, in accordance with the laws of Moses and Israel.

The 'get' must be witnessed by two Jews over the age of thirteen not related to the husband or the wife or to each other, and its issue is controlled by the religious court. Divorced people are encouraged to remarry.

▼ **Divorce has no stigma (bad effects) in Judaism, though it is regarded as unfortunate. One book on Judaism says: 'Jewish divorce [should] be as warm, human, and emotionally involving as possible.' Do you think this could be the case or not? Write down your opinions.**

Sikhism

Religious life and family life

Sikhism is a community religion. The family is extremely important. Sikhs are not encouraged to retreat from life nor to become hermits; their main roles in life are as part of a family. Guru Nanak, the first Guru (or spiritual teacher) of the Sikh religion, said that people can reach God while living in the world. The demands of home and family should be met to the best of one's ability.

> Nanak I have met the true Guru and my union with God is accomplished;
> Salvation can be achieved even while men are laughing, playing, wearing fine clothes and eating.
> [Guru Arjan, Gujari ki Var]

A wedding in a Sikh gurdwara. The bride and bridegroom are facing the holy book called the Guru Granth Sahib. The person sitting behind it is called the 'Granthi'. Can you see the rich cloths lying around the book? These are used to cover the book when the ceremonies are finished. The book is honoured like an important person. Describe what else you see

Relations between husband and wife

Marriage is usually arranged or 'assisted' by the two families, though the assent of those being married is needed. The marriage is not just between the couple but between the two families, especially since the bride will go to live in the bridegroom's family home. The symbol of marriage is given spiritual significance. The two souls of husband and wife are said to become one.

Guru Amar Das, one of the Ten Gurus, gave the following advice on marriage:

 The bride should know no other man
Except her husband, so the Guru ordains.
She alone is of good family,
She alone shines with light
Who is adorned with the love of her husband.
There is only one way to the heart of the beloved:
To be humble and true and to do his bidding . . .
They are not man and wife who have only physical contact;
Only they are truly wedded who have one spirit in two bodies.
Another person's property, another man's wife,
Talking ill of another, poison one's life.
Like the touch of a poisonous snake
Is the touch of another man's wife.

The husband should love and respect his wife, recognise her individuality and equality. He should be kind and gentle to her, guide and support her.

The wife should show her respect and loyalty for her husband, sharing life's joys and sorrows.

Men and women are regarded as equal in Sikhism. Wives are regarded highly and they have an important role in the home. A Sikh woman should only marry a Sikh man.

The Sikh marriage hymns, the Lavan, are read out and sung during the ceremony. They describe the development of marital love between husband and wife and, at the same time, the love and longing of the soul for God. This is part of verse four:

 By singing the Lord's praises
I have attained my heart's desire.
God has completed this marriage
And the bride's heart rejoices in His Name.

Contraception and divorce

There is no specific guidance on contraception, so most Sikhs will normally follow the trend of the society in which they live. Divorce is rare and is against the principles of the Sikh religion.

▼　'They are not man and wife who have only physical contact; Only they are truly wedded who have *one spirit in two bodies*.' Discuss whether this is possible or whether this is just an ideal. Does it mean two equal partners or one subservient to the other?

▼ General assignments

▼ **Look back at the sections on 'Religious life and family life'. Do all the religions consider marriage and family to be the best way of life? Discuss what you find. Does any religion not regard marriage as important?**

Although these six religions have different views on marriage there are many similar views which tell us what a religious view of marriage might be. We could say these are:

1 A *social* relationship which brings together different families.
2 A *loving* relationship which is either the reason for marriage or the basis upon which the future relationship will develop. It implies a shared set of values as well as a strong commitment between the couple.
3 A *sexual and biological* relationship which will provide children who will add to the relationship between the parents. It is also a pleasurable relationship, though the emphasis differs between religions. It reflects the strong sexual drive in human beings and harnesses it in a binding public relationship between two people.
4 An *economic* relationship in which the bride and groom share their property, their home and their possessions with each other.

▼ **Look again at these four aspects of marriage. Consider them in a small group and make notes on the following:**
   a) Do any of these statements need any further explanation? Add to them if you think they do.
   b) Has any aspect of marriage been left out? Give your reasons if you think it has.

▼ **Select a quotation from each religion that you think best sums up that religion's attitude to marriage. Learn it by heart.**

▼ **Look at the sections that describe the relations between husband and wife. Are husband and wife always equal? Do they have the same roles in marriage? Choose two religions and write a paragraph to show the similarities or differences in the roles of husband and wife.**

▼ **Look back over this chapter and make a brief note on what each religion's position is as regards contraception. You could make a chart with the headings: Religions that allow artificial contraception; Religions that allow contraception if the woman's health is affected; Religions that let the individual decide. (It is worth remembering, however, that not all followers of a religion do what their leaders, or sacred texts, require. Many use their own initiative to do what they believe is best for their family at the time.)**

▼ **Discuss if all these religions allow divorce. Do they have the same attitudes to divorce? And the same attitudes to remarriage?**

▼ **Choose one religion and without looking back at the chapter, write down what its attitude is to: a) marriage, b) divorce, c) contraception. Then look back and see if you were correct.**

This prayer is sometimes used at a Jewish wedding:

66 Lord, who taught men and women to help and serve each other in marriage, and lead each other into happiness, bless this covenant of affection, these promises of truth. Protect and care for the bridegroom and bride as they go through life together. May they be loving companions, secure in their devotion which deepens with the passing years. In their respect and honour for each other may they find their peace, and in their affection and tenderness their happiness. May your presence be in their home and in their hearts.

▼ **Make a list of the major issues in this prayer. Does it sum up the central meaning of marriage for these six religions or not? Would you add anything to it? Share your opinion with the rest of your group.**

2 ▼ Abortion and Medical Ethics

▼ Introduction

Most of us take medical treatment for granted. If we are ill we go to the doctor's. The doctor tries to diagnose the problem and may prescribe some medicine. If the illness is more serious, or it isn't clear what is wrong, the doctor will arrange for tests at a hospital. If the illness is severe enough it might involve a stay in hospital so that an operation can be performed.

Behind this simple picture is the very complicated world of modern medical technology and the ethical problems which result from it. The newspaper headlines show some of these dilemmas. This chapter looks at some of the issues.

Research

How do doctors know that drugs and operations will work? All drugs have first been tested on animals. Many operations have first been carried out on animals. Some people say that all such research should be stopped because it is cruel and unnecessary. Others say that the experiments are vital and that the animals are very well cared for.

▼ **Do animals have the same rights as humans? Or is human life more important than animal life? Write down your thoughts about this.**

Embryo pioneers give women with leukaemia chance of baby

Creating life

Scientists can take an egg from a woman and the sperm from a man and mix them together in a glass dish to create a living human embryo. If this is transferred into a woman's womb it can develop into a baby. In order to do this, research has to take place on human embryos, and some will be thrown away.

▼ **When does life begin? Does life begin at conception or does it begin at a later stage? Write down what you think.**

Another problem concerns 'genetic engineering'. This goes beyond creating life in a 'test-tube'. It means that scientists can actually alter the genes of any living thing – plants, animals and humans. Genes are what we inherit from our parents. They make us what we are and what our children will be. This technique can cure genetic diseases. It can also create new kinds of cows or sheep. Human genes are used to modify animals. Scientists could in theory modify humans – to create people of 'superior intelligence' or appearance.

Patients at the brink of death being kept alive for transplants

Sustaining life

Some badly injured people can be kept alive in hospital through the use of life-support machines. There may come a moment when the doctors feel that nothing more can be done for the patient. Usually the next of kin will have to make this decision. They must trust in the doctors' advice.

▼   **When does life end? Do you think this is an easy or a difficult thing to decide? Write down what you think.**

Doctor struck off for using kidneys from paid donors

Organ transplants happen quite frequently nowadays. But they can be very expensive. Should there be fewer transplants in order to free money and resources to help those with less serious ailments? There have been recent cases of people being pressurised into donating one of their kidneys for money. Is it wrong to receive money for this? With all the new technology, such as life-support machines, might a doctor be pressurised into turning a machine off if it is known someone needs one of the patient's organs? Doctors may also have to face the decision on whom to treat when there is limited money, or not enough donated organs.

▼   **If there are only four kidney machines but fifteen patients need them urgently, how would you make the decision on which four to treat? Write down how you think you might decide.**

Doctors and nurses say they decide which babies will die

'If you really love me, help me to die'

Destroying life

Should badly deformed babies, or people suffering from painful and incurable diseases, who are only kept alive because of modern technology, be allowed to die with dignity, or should they be kept alive at all costs? Doctors must try to preserve life, so how can they approve of abortion? Are the rights of an unborn child more important than the health and rights of the woman?

▼   **Many people, including the doctors themselves, are worried about the advances of medical science. Sometimes the advance has gone faster than the public can understand. Discuss in a group what you think. Are you concerned about these advances and think there should be more controls, or do you feel that there are enough controls already and that all medical progress must be a good thing?**

▼ Abortion

Abortion is simply the ending of pregnancy before birth. It can happen naturally, when it is called 'spontaneous' abortion, or a 'miscarriage'. Most conceptions abort in this way. It can also be made to happen deliberately. This is what people usually mean by 'abortion'. Deliberately expelling a foetus has been practised for over 3,000 years. Most abortions in Britain take place outside marriage.

It is a very emotional subject and people, countries and religions have strong feelings for and against abortion. In Britain and elsewhere, arguments rage about whether abortion should be legal. If it is to be legal, up to what stage in pregnancy should it be allowed? Should abortion be difficult to get or should it be available on demand or request?

The 1967 Abortion Act

Abortion in Britain is not available 'on demand'. Until 1967 all abortions were illegal unless the mother's life was in danger. Some women had abortions in hospital if they could show that having a baby would damage their health. If they had the money some private clinics carried out the (illegal) operation. If they were poor they had to visit often unqualified persons with the risk of serious infection or death. Thousands did visit these 'back-street' clinics. Many suffered permanent ill health as a result. A number died.

In order to stop these illegal abortions, the 1967 Abortion Act made abortion legal in England, Wales and Scotland in certain circumstances:

1 Two doctors have to sign the certificate giving approval for the abortion.
2 There are four conditions for carrying out an abortion:
   a) if the mother's life is at risk
   b) if there is a risk of injury to the woman's mental or physical health
   c) if there is a risk that another child could be a risk to the mental or physical health of existing children
   d) if there is a substantial risk that if the child was born it would be seriously physically or mentally handicapped.

The Act did not give a time limit, but it was linked to a 1929 Act that made it a criminal offence to destroy the life of any child capable of being born alive. This was believed to be at 28 weeks.

It is up to the doctors to decide whether any of these things will happen. A doctor can refuse to give approval if it is against his or her conscience. One doctor's opinion about the risks mentioned above will often differ from another doctor's. It is still easier to get an abortion if a woman has money and goes to a private clinic, than it is if she tries to get one on the National Health Service.

Time limit

In April 1990 MPs reduced the time limit for abortion to 24 weeks. Since the 1967 Act, medical advances have meant that a small percentage of babies born at 24 weeks can survive. There is no time limit, however, if the woman's health is seriously at risk, or if the foetus is seriously handicapped.

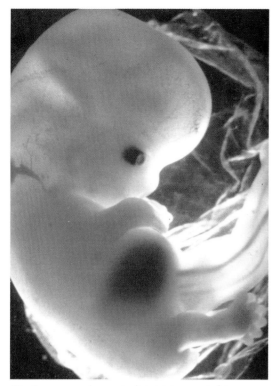

*The human embryo at about seven weeks,
measuring about 3 cm long. The arms and
legs have begun to form – the toes are
visible*

This is a foetus about five months old

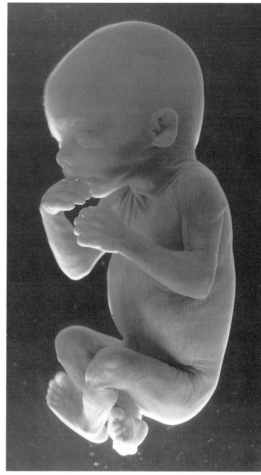

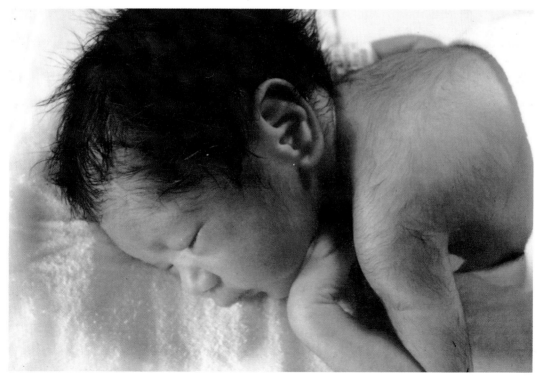

*This baby was born two months premature (at about 32 weeks) and is in an incubator. Notice
the hair on its body which later disappears*

▼ Abortion – some statistics

The most common reason given for abortion in Britain is 'risk of injury to the woman's mental or physical health'. The table below shows the reasons given for the 162,454 abortions carried out in England and Wales in 1981. (In 1987 the total number was 174,276.)

Reason given on form	Number of times this was mentioned in 1981
1 Risk to life of the mother	787
2 Risk of injury to health of mother	158,499
3 Risk to the mother's other children	20,707
4 Risk of the baby being handicapped	2,052
(In 1987 this category had fallen to	1,826)

The USA allows abortion on request up to 12 weeks, though each State has the right to decide on this, so it is more difficult in some States than in others. In 1988 there were 1.6 million abortions – about one-third of the total number of registered conceptions.

In France abortion is available on request up to 10 weeks. About 1.5% of women have abortions. An 'abortion pill' was launched in 1989 and many thousands of women each year use it to have very early abortions.

The Netherlands allows abortion on request up to 24 weeks. It has the lowest abortion rate in the West – 0.6% of women have abortions.

In Eastern Europe, where contraceptives are difficult to find, abortion is the main method of birth control. Although accurate figures are difficult to obtain, it is estimated that 18% of women have abortions in the USSR.

In Scotland doctors follow the practice in England and Wales. About 0.75% of women have abortions. In 1987 there were 9,351 abortions.

In the Republic of Ireland, all abortion is illegal, and so is giving women advice about it. However, in 1988 almost 4,000 Irish women had abortions in England. Unofficially there were perhaps thousands more. (Abortion is also illegal in Northern Ireland.)

In England and Wales about 1.5% of women have abortions. In 1987 less than a quarter of registered conceptions ended in abortion. Most of these abortions (87%) were carried out on women under 13 weeks pregnant. Less than 2% were on women more than 20 weeks pregnant. Over two-fifths of the abortions were carried out on (mostly unmarried) women under the age of twenty.

In England and Wales there were almost three million legal abortions in the twenty years between 1968 (when the Abortion Act came into force) and 1988. Of these, 130 were performed in an emergency situation in order to save the life of a pregnant woman. About a third were carried out on women who were visitors or not resident in England and Wales.

▼ List the reasons why you think the 1967 Abortion Act was considered necessary. Include your opinion on whether the four conditions for abortion are enough (see page 46).

▼ Below are some statements. Based on the information you have from the 1967 Abortion Act on page 46, do you think they *allow* or *forbid* a legal abortion? Remember to give reasons for your answer.
   a) Tests showed the baby was likely to be born physically handicapped.
   b) Tests showed that the baby was a boy and the parents wanted a girl.
   c) The woman became pregnant by being raped.
   d) The parents were very poor and already had a large family.
   e) The parents simply didn't want another baby.

In April 1990 the House of Commons agreed to reduce the upper time limit to 24 weeks. In the debate Sir David Steel MP said:

❝ If this were a less male-dominated House, we would have spent less time debating abortion and more time discussing family planning facilities.

▼ Look at the statistics for the different countries. In a group decide why the abortion rate appears to be different in each country. What might be the reasons for this?

Some people are opposed to almost all abortions. Among them is MP David Alton, shown here before unsuccessfully presenting a Bill to Parliament in 1988. He wanted to shorten the abortion time limit to 18 weeks. What point is he trying to make here? What can you see in the background?

▼ When does life begin?

Babies are formed in the mother's womb and take on human characteristics after only a few weeks. The following are extracts from *Puffball*, a novel by Fay Weldon:

> 66 Six weeks. The limb buds of the foetus began to show and the tail to disappear. The heart formed within the chest cavity and began the activity which was to last till the end of its days.
>
> 66 Eleven weeks. Liffey's [the name of the mother] baby had eyes beneath solid eyelids, a nose and rudimentary hands and feet. It weighed ten grams.
>
> 66 Thirteen weeks. . . . the foetus was three inches long. The baby's face was properly formed: its body curled in an attitude of docility; resting, waiting, listening, growing.
>
> 66 [Sixteen weeks] The baby weighed five ounces and was six inches long. It had limbs with working joints, and fingers and toes, each with its completing nail. It was clearly male.
>
> 66 Eighteen weeks. The doctor laid a stethoscope to Liffey's swelling abdomen, and she heard the beat of her baby's heart. 160 a minute.
>
> 66 Twenty weeks. The baby moved, there could be no doubt of it.

The moment at about twenty weeks when the baby moves used to be called the 'quickening' and in some religions was the moment when the unborn baby had 'life'.

For most people, whether they are religious or not, an important question is: When does life begin? Every baby in the womb is unique. Perhaps 80% of conceptions will abort 'spontaneously', but the rest will grow and be born as unique human beings.

Some people believe that because of this uniqueness life begins at conception. This means that right from the very moment when the sperm fertilises the egg the embryo has the same rights as anyone else. They believe that to destroy the embryo is the same as murder.

Other people, with equal concern, argue that the state of the embryo in the early weeks is so unlike that of the newborn child that to abort it is not murder. They believe that human life does not begin at the moment of conception. For example, the egg only embeds in the lining of the womb after about 7 to 10 days. Then it takes another week to be firmly attached. (This is the 14-day period after fertilisation during which many people believe research on embryos is right.)

Some people say that the decision on whether to abort or not should depend on whether the foetus could survive on its own outside the womb. They argue that abortion should be legal if the birth of the foetus would cause it to die. But, as medical science develops, it is possible to keep very young babies alive. Currently five per cent of babies born at 24 weeks will survive if intensive care equipment is available.

▼ **Read the extracts from Fay Weldon's novel again. Write down what your feelings are when you read her account. Do you think 'life' has begun or not by twenty weeks?**

▼   **When does life begin? Look again at the notes you made earlier in the chapter. Add to them or alter them if you wish, then compare your opinions and reasons with others.**

A couple with their five-week-old baby who was conceived by in vitro fertilisation (see page 58). Without research on embryos, IVF would not have been possible. Many of those who think life begins at conception believe that research on embryos is wrong

▼ A woman's right to choose?

Abortion is never taken lightly. It can be very distressing for the mother, the doctors and nurses. The arguments are to do with the rights of the *woman* against the rights of the *unborn child*. Which should be considered the more important? Below are some points and quotations on both sides.

Rights of the unborn child

Many people are concerned about the rights of the unborn child, this includes many doctors and nurses. It cannot speak for itself but it clearly has a 'life' of some sort, though arguments take place about the nature of that life.

Here are some of the views often expressed :

The baby is a person from conception. It has rights from that moment. It depends on the mother but is also distinct from her. Its life must be protected.

Unborn children have unique personalities. It is impossible to know how valuable their lives might be.

If abortion is acceptable, where do we draw the line? Murder is murder.

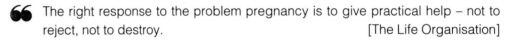 The right response to the problem pregnancy is to give practical help – not to reject, not to destroy. [The Life Organisation]

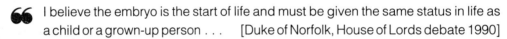 I believe the embryo is the start of life and must be given the same status in life as a child or a grown-up person . . . [Duke of Norfolk, House of Lords debate 1990]

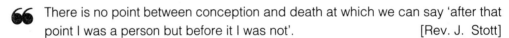 There is no point between conception and death at which we can say 'after that point I was a person but before it I was not'. [Rev. J. Stott]

Rights of the woman

Many people argue that it is every woman's right to choose whether or not to have a child.

Here are some of their arguments:

Women have a right to control their own fertility. The foetus is in the woman's body. The woman must make the final decision. It is her life that will be most affected – her health, her freedom. No one wants abortion but it is better than misery or poverty.

Legal abortions early in pregnancy are easy and safe, safer than childbirth. If women didn't have to wait for doctors' permissions, abortions could be done more quickly and safely than they are at present.

Human life does not begin at the moment of conception. The foetus has no life of its own apart from the mother. It feels nothing. To kill it is not 'murder'.

No woman should be forced to have a child because of rape. Every child should be a wanted child. Every mother should be a willing mother.

 What women want is a real choice between having a safe, legal abortion if they don't want children, and having an adequate standard of living so that they can bring up the children they do want with dignity. [National Abortion Campaign]

❝ Anti-abortionists have no right to impose their morality on the rest of us. They have no right to say that they know better than the woman concerned what choices she can make about her life. [National Abortion Campaign]

▼ **Organise a small debate in a group where the the rights of the woman and of the unborn child are argued.**

▼ **Write an article as if you were writing for the local newspaper, putting the arguments for and against abortion. You can express you own opinion, but support it with reasons.**

Judge rules on test-tube case that split a nation

WIFE WINS HER FIGHT FOR FROZEN 'BABIES'

HER CASE

● MARY SUE argued that the embryos were human beings and not just property. She claimed she had the right to have a baby with or without Junior's consent.

● The embryos are part of my body, she said – not just property jointly owned by me and Junior.

● Now the judge has given her temporary custody of the embryos so that she can implant them in her womb and have a baby.

● He agreed with her case that the embryos are not property, and in a historic decision said life begins at conception.

● Mary Sue has not yet finally won her case. Junior has vowed to appeal within the next 30 days.

WIFE: Mary Sue

HIS CASE

● JUNIOR said no one had the right to make him a father without his consent. He said Mary Sue could always get herself fertilised with someone else's sperm if she still wanted a test-tube baby.

● He added that he would dread the idea of walking down the street in ten years' time and bumping into his own child, whom he would not know.

● Junior said he would rather leave the embryos in cold storage than bring them into the world without two parents to look after them.

● Many people agreed with him. And after the judge's ruling yesterday he told reporters: "I still do not feel that these embryos are human. They've potential for life but are just genetic material."

HUSBAND: Junior

This couple's sperm and eggs were fertilised in a laboratory and then frozen. They then divorced. Do you think the argument about the frozen embryos at this trial in the USA helps in the discussion about 'rights'?

▼ Opinions on abortion

Look at the following comments on how some people feel about the issue of abortion.

I believe the choice to have or not to have a child should be left to the individual woman. But I also think a woman must be made fully aware that what is at stake is not a clump of inert cells but the beginning of human life.

Hardly any attention has been paid to men who suffer as a result of abortion. It is not our masculinity that is threatened or conquered: it is our feelings that we have done wrong.

I can think of one very compelling case in particular where a woman had every good reason for an abortion. She was forty-one years of age when she discovered she was pregnant for the fourth time. Her two oldest children were fully grown teenagers, and her third child was ten. Her husband was in his sixties. Her elderly mother was living with her, and ailing. Times were hard. There was a war on, and rations were modest. She really was in despair as to know how she could cope with another child. She wept for weeks when the pregnancy was confirmed, and felt deeply depressed . . . she gritted her teeth and carried on.
The baby was born in due course. And that baby was me. . . . I am very glad I was born, and what is more important, so is she.

No woman has the right to kill. Women don't really want abortions . . . To go through an abortion is the saddest thing and only a woman who has, can tell you.

In these days, when everyone is anxious for women to have the right to be independent, they should have the right to decide what happens to their bodies. Women *do* want abortions.

Although nurses and often the general public would prefer abortions – for social reasons, particularly – not to take place, they can often see that life for the mother and the baby would be less than ideal if the pregnancy continued.

People want 'quality babies' and are prepared to be selective and reject the imperfect.

▼   If society only has 'quality babies' does that mean we want a 'perfect race'?
Does it mean we care less about those who are not 'perfect'? Discuss this in
a group and note down your answers.

▼   Look carefully at the quotations. In groups each person choose *one* passage
which they find interesting or reflects their own point of view. Discuss the
passages in the group and note down everyone's point of view.

▼   Is abortion only a woman's issue? What rights does the father have? Prepare
an interview in which a couple are discussing the pros and cons of abortion.
Remember to include each person's feelings.

▼   Amniocentesis is a test offered to pregnant women over 37 years of age. It
can only be done at about 16 weeks of pregnancy. It can tell whether the
unborn baby is likely to suffer a serious abnormality such as Down's
syndrome. Write down how you would make a decision for or against
abortion if you knew your child would be born with Down's syndrome. (About
1,500 – 2,000 women each year in the UK have an abortion for this reason.)

*These youngsters were born with the handicap known as Down's syndrome and are here
doing a life skills course*

▼

▼ The technology of birth

There are no precise statistics concerning couples who are unable to have a child but it is thought to be about one in six. Some of these couples may not want to have children, but others can be deeply upset by their inability to conceive a child . The most common reason for childlessness in couples is the infertility of the man. About one in 20 men is thought to be infertile.

▼ **Do you believe each couple has a right to a child, even in an overpopulated world? Should the best medical research make it possible for them to have one? This is a good topic for debate.**

Artificial insemination

This is the name for the technique which places a man's semen in a fertile woman's cervix other than by intercourse. There are two sorts of 'AI':

AIH

If the male partner's sperm is fertile it will be placed in the woman's cervix, with an instrument, at the most fertile time of her cycle. This can be carried out by a doctor but it is quite normal for the couple to do this themselves. The term for this is *Artificial Insemination Husband* (AIH). This method allows the male to have some sperm frozen in case, after a vasectomy, he and his partner decide they would like children.

AID

Artificial Insemination Donor is used if the male partner is infertile or if he has a hereditary fault which will be passed on to the child. In these cases the sperm used is from an anonymous donor, although doctors do try to 'match' the donor to the father (e.g. height, intelligence). The method of insemination will be the same.

The British law at the time of writing says that the child produced as a result of AID is technically 'illegitimate'. It is, however, normal for the mother to put her partner's name on the birth certificate (if she has one). In AIH the child of course is the actual child of both parents, but in AID a third person, the male donor, is the natural father of the child.

One aspect of AID is that one donor could 'father' a number of children who, in turn, may conceive with each other. This might lead to genetic problems. The Warnock Report of 1984 recognised this and recommended that all AID babies should be registered and that no donor should provide more than 10 children. It also recommended that AID offspring should be legitimate and that the identity of the donor be kept secret.

▼ **Should AID be freely available to all women or only those with husbands or a steady partner? Write down your opinion and then share it with others.**

▼ **One definition of a 'father' is one who fertilises the woman's ovum (egg). However, is a 'father' more than this? Would a husband easily accept a child born by means of AID? Write down your view of this and discuss it.**

Surrogate motherhood

If the woman is infertile or if it would be dangerous for her to bear a child, another woman might agree to bear the child for her and hand it over at birth. She might be paid money for this. Either the embryo (fertilised in a laboratory) is placed in the surrogate mother's womb (this is called 'total surrogacy'), or she uses artificial insemination to place the man's semen near her cervix. In this case she would be the natural mother. (This is called 'partial surrogacy'.)

There have been a number of cases in the newspapers about this in recent years. The pregnant woman can become attached to the unborn child and not wish to hand it over at birth. If she does hand it over, its loss might have a deep emotional impact on her and her family. If it is handicapped, the 'commissioning' couple might refuse to take it.

In the United States surrogacy is more frequent and it is legal for agencies to make money out of arranging it. In Britain, however, it is against the law to make a profit out of surrogacy. Voluntary agencies, however, are allowed.

In March 1990, the British Medical Association said that doctors should be allowed to help couples over the surrogacy issue, as long as they followed certain guidelines. One guideline is that the identity of the surrogate mother should not be known to the couple.

▼ **Why do you think the BMA says that the identity of the surrogate mother should be kept secret? Discuss this in groups. Do you think this is right – both for the couple and the child?**

In law the mother of such a child is the surrogate mother, even if the egg was not hers but was donated. The genetic parents are only seen as foster parents, and they may have to adopt the child. The courts might decide, however, that they are not suitable parents for the child.

❝ I am very happily married; the one thing missing is a child. I have known my husband for six years. Until last year I wouldn't marry him because I couldn't have a child. Time is running out for me and surrogacy is the only way we can have a child of our own. [A woman who does not have a womb because of cancer]

▼ **In small groups discuss whether you think a surrogate mother should be able to keep the baby she gives birth to if she wishes.**

▼ **Should surrogate motherhood be banned? The Government does not think so. Do you agree? List arguments for and against the opinion.**

The woman is a surrogate mother for this couple. What are the problems which could arise from this method of having children?

In vitro fertilisation (IVF)

A popular name for this is 'test-tube babies' (*in vitro* means 'in glass'). This method can be used where AIH and AID have failed or because the woman's fallopian tubes are blocked. Sperm and eggs are taken from the couple and fertilised in a laboratory in a glass dish. Once the embryos have developed to the eight-cell stage (at two days old), two or three may be replaced in the womb of the mother (in the hope that one will implant). So conception, in the sense of the sperm fertilising the egg, takes place outside the woman's body.

Since 1978 this method has been used world-wide. Thousands of babies have been born as a result of it. Sometimes twins or triplets might result but there is not a high success rate of even one baby.

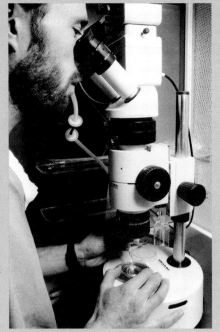

In vitro fertilisation, or IVF. The technician is using an optical microscope. The dish contains a mixture of human sperm and eggs (the sperm have just been added)

Apart from the couple's egg and sperm being used, it is also possible to mix an egg from another woman with that of the male partner's sperm, and to place this in the wife's womb. This is called 'egg donation'. If the husband is also infertile, both the semen and the egg could be donated, mixed in the laboratory and then placed in the wife's womb. This is called 'embryo donation'. The child would then have four parents!

Embryo research

In vitro fertilisation only exists because of research on embryos in the laboratory. In order to do this research, eggs are collected from the woman and each one is mixed in a laboratory with the man's sperm to produce an embryo. Some will be replaced in the woman, but not all. The spare ones can be kept alive for several days, and some may be frozen for later research. Embryos can also be created if a woman about to be sterilised donates eggs. A drug can make a woman produce twenty or more eggs at a time instead of one.

Many people have strong views about using human embryos for research.

For research

Research in Britain is only allowed during the first 14 days of the embryo. This is the time before an embryo is attached to the womb. Some people say it is not a true individual until then, for example the cells will only split to form twins after 14 days. The embryo, these people say, therefore cannot have a 'soul' until after this occurs.

Research can also help people who risk passing on genetic disorders. The sex of the child can be known from the embryo in the laboratory. This means that doctors can control the passing on of genetic disease which might only be passed on to a boy and not a girl. So, for example, only a female embryo might be replaced in the mother. Also, an embryo that has a defect would not be replaced, for example if it would mean the child would have thalassaemia or cystic fibrosis. Future research might also cure such disorders. This involves genetic engineering, which creates more ethical problems.

 Unless we ourselves have handicapped children, we really cannot know what it means. Yes, of course there is love. There is more love because the child is handicapped. But there is also a great hardship, which none of us would want to take on ourselves. [Lord Ennals, House of Lords debate 1990]

Research on embryos can lead to ways to treat male infertility. It has also led to the discovery of a contraceptive vaccine.

The medical profession is, however, concerned about the rapid advance of medical science and believe that their work should have strict legal controls.

Against research

Opponents of research say that even the earliest embryo has a soul. Life begins when sperm meets egg.

 I cannot accept that man has a right to take life, bottle it, put it on a shelf, play with it and destroy it. [Lord Rawlinson, House of Lords debate 1990]

The practice of women donating eggs for research creates ethical problems. It could lead to women donating eggs for money.

It is not known what the long-term effects might be of fertility drugs on women and their babies.

Without proper guidance, embryos might simply be experimented on to 'see what happens'. Researchers already mix human sperm with an animal's eggs, and can inject a human egg with an animal's sperm. Many find this horrific and are worried that this might result in a 'cross species' of human and animal, although scientists say this is impossible. Or they could produce embryos of identical twins and use one of them for experimentation. These possibilities are regarded as 'unnatural' and as manipulating the human race. Many religious people believe that research wrongly places the responsibility for the creation of human beings upon doctors and scientists and not upon God.

The British Government said:

 It will be a criminal offence to carry out any procedures on a human embryo other than those aiming at preparing the embryo for transfer to the uterus.

▼ **Prepare a class debate on the use of human embryos for medical research. Note carefully all the arguments for and against.**

▼ Organ transplants

Many people today carry a donor card. They are found in many shops as well as in doctors' surgeries. They request that after death some, or all, parts of the body may be transplanted into another person.

The best-known transplants are heart and kidney transplants. If a person has a damaged heart, it can be replaced by an undamaged one from a donor. Eyes, liver and pancreas can also be transplanted after death. In the case of a kidney transplant, the donor may be living because it is possible to live with only one kidney. This is the same with a bone marrow transplant to combat a form of cancer, though this is usually best if it comes from a close relative.

The major medical problem with all transplants is that the body wants to reject the new 'foreign' part. The patient has to be given drugs to stop this rejection and it is the rejection of the new organ which causes most deaths. The first heart transplant was carried out in 1967, and in the 1960s and 1970s made newspaper headlines, but they have become more common today.

▼ **What would your feelings be if you were asked to give parts of your body in a transplant? Would you have the same feelings if you had to give permission for a relation's organs to be used? Write an account of how you might feel if a doctor asked you (or a relative) to be a donor.**

Problems with donating organs

Transplant jury to vet live donors

Donor's consent 'is ethical key'

It seems a good idea to use organs from one person to give life to another, but some people argue that live donors can be put under pressure to donate an organ when they don't really want to.

This is only half the problem. The use of organs from dead people raises the question of when death has happened. Is a person dead if their heart is still beating?

You will hear the phrase 'brain death'. This is when a machine records that there is no brain activity – so all evidence of personality, mind and thought has gone. 'Clinical death' is when the heart and lungs have ceased to function. But machines can keep a patient 'alive' clinically after brain death has happened. So when is a person dead – or alive?

Two years before this photograph was taken, Liam Cuthbert was dying and was given a heart transplant. Here he is at nine, alive and well, with the then Sports Minister Colin Moynihan

There may be, it is argued, a temptation for a doctor to keep a prospective donor 'alive' on a machine until the last possible moment. Might the doctor diagnose death in order to match up with the needs of a transplant? It is now necessary for the doctor who certifies death not to be connected with the transplant medical team.

▼   **Transplants cost a lot of money. In a group discuss whether you think it is worth spending such a lot of money on one person.**

▼   **When do you decide if a person is dead? Write down how you would define 'death'. It may help you to look up how you defined 'life'.**

▼ Euthanasia

This word literally means 'to die well' or 'a good death', though nowadays it means causing such a death to happen, usually because someone is suffering from a painful and incurable disease or injury.

Voluntary euthanasia

Some people who know that they are incurable want to die painlessly and with dignity. This might involve taking a drug, or it might mean being detached from a life-support machine. Medical techniques can keep people alive for much longer than they used to. It is, however, against the law to help someone to die, either by giving them a drug, or by turning off a machine, even if the person requests this. There are people and societies who want the law changed but it is unlikely to happen. One organisation is the Voluntary Euthanasia Society, which argues that those with incurable illnesses should be able to choose when to die and that doctors should be allowed to help them.

In 1969 Lord Raglan tried to persuade the House of Lords to help make voluntary euthanasia legal. He failed. In 1972 he announced that he had changed his mind. People who had disagreed with him in 1969 pointed out that those who died, unlike him, would have no second chance. Another argument against voluntary euthanasia is that a person might recover. It is also possible that people, especially elderly people, could be pressurised into agreeing to it.

The following is an extract from a play, *Whose Life is it Anyway?* After a serious accident, Ken is paralysed from the neck down and is faced with total dependence on a life-support machine. He claims the right to make his own decisions about his life. He wants to be discharged from hospital. If he is, he will die within a week.

KEN: Of course I want to live but as far as I am concerned I'm dead already. I merely require the doctors to recognise the fact. I cannot accept this condition constitutes life in any real sense at all. . . . I am not asking anyone to kill me. I am only asking to be discharged from this hospital.

JUDGE: It comes to the same thing.

KEN: Then that proves my point; not just the fact that I will spend the rest of my life in hospital, but that whilst I am here, everything is geared just to keeping my brain active, with no real possibility of it ever being able to direct anything. As far as I can see, that is an act of deliberate cruelty.

JUDGE: Surely, it would be more cruel if society let people die, when it could, with some effort, keep them alive.

KEN: No, not *more* cruel, *just* as cruel. . . . The cruelty doesn't reside in saving someone or allowing them to die. It resides in the fact that the choice is removed from the man concerned. . . . It is a question of dignity. . . . I find the hospital's persistent effort to maintain this shadow of life an indignity and it's inhumane. . . . Dignity starts with choice. If I choose to live, it would be appalling if society killed me. If I choose to die, it is equally appalling if society keeps me alive.

▼ **Write down Ken's arguments in your own words.**

Compulsory euthanasia

This is sometimes also called 'mercy killing'. Someone who is seriously ill may not be able to express a wish whether to die or not.

It has been estimated that over 20% of hospital beds are occupied by the elderly who are unable to wash and feed themselves or speak to people. Some argue that these people would surely prefer to die quietly and painlessly and not be kept alive by medical science. Other people have been so badly injured in accidents that they are only kept alive by life-support machines. Relatives may be caused more unhappiness by seeing their loved one kept alive in this way than if they were allowed to die with dignity.

The hospice movement

Here is a poem written by a dying patient in a hospital:

 I huddle warm inside my corner bed,
Watching the other patients sipping tea.
I wonder why I'm so long getting well,
And why it is no one will talk to me.

The nurses are so kind. They brush my hair
On days I feel too ill to read or sew.
I smile and chat, try not to show my fear
They cannot tell me what I want to know.

The visitors come in. I see their eyes
Become embarrassed as they pass my bed.
'What lovely flowers' they say, then hurry on
In case their faces show what can't be said.

The chaplain passes on his weekly round
With friendly smile and calm, untroubled brow.
He speaks with deep sincerity of life.
I'd like to speak of death, but don't know how.

The surgeon comes, with student retinue
Mutters to Sister, deaf to my silent plea.
I want to tell this dread I feel inside,
But they are all too kind to talk to me.

A hospice is a special kind of hospital that cares for the dying. Modern hospices began in the late 1960s and usually have a Christian foundation. Although many of the nurses may be Christian, the patients can be of any religion or none. The staff not only look after the patients, they also help the relatives to cope with the death. The atmosphere is a warm and caring one, where the patient and family are encouraged to talk about dying, to feel at home and see each other as often as possible. The staff relieve the patient of as much of the pain as possible.

▼   **Helen House is a well-known hospice for children in Oxford. You could make a folder on its work, or on the work of Dame Cicely Saunders, who founded the first modern hospice in London in 1967.**

▼ Vivisection and animal rights

Vivisection is the use of live animals for experiments. Throughout the world, animals are used in medical research to test drugs and operations. Animals are also used in other kinds of research to test such things as cosmetics and toiletries, food additives, agricultural chemicals, dyes and household cleaners, to see how these might affect humans and ensure that they are safe.

It is difficult to estimate the numbers of animals used in this way. In 1876 it is thought there were under 1,000 animals being used for research in the UK. The figure today is between three and four million. Most of these animals will be destroyed after the experiments.

 In the two major areas of farming and experimentation alone, approximately 100 billion animals are killed every year. Use of experimental animals in the United States is . . . estimated in the region of 70 to a 120 million. Worldwide the total is probably somewhere around 500 million.

Do animals have rights?

We know today that animals can feel pain and can suffer. The important argument is about whether we ought to care for animals so that they avoid unnecessary suffering (the *Welfare* view), or whether animals actually have the same rights as humans. This *Rights* view says that we have all developed from the same source. Both animals and humans feel pain, hunger and fear. The animal rights movement is said to be the fastest growing reform movement. Those who believe in the rights movement are not only against experimenting on animals, many also believe that meat eating, zoos, hunting, even keeping pets is wrong.

One problem is, should all animals be treated in the same way? Is it all right to kill a rat because it is a pest, but not right to kill a fox by hunting it? Is it right to experiment on a mouse, but not on a dog or a chimpanzee? Is it right to breed animals, like pigs, for food, but not right to breed animals for experiments?

Those who do *not* believe animals have the same rights as humans might say that just as the suffering of a dog is worse than the suffering of a worm, so the suffering of a human being is worse than that of a dog.

Medical research

 If one, or even a dozen animals had to suffer experiments in order to save thousands, I would think it right . . . that they should do so.

[Peter Singer, *Practical Ethics*]

Animals have been experimented on for over 2,000 years. Without research on animals we would have very little scientific knowledge. Research on animals in the past has meant that we know about blood circulation, the function of the nervous system, the skeleton and the brain. Epidemic diseases would not have been understood or conquered. New types of operations depend on experimenting on animals first. If animal research is not allowed for multiple sclerosis, kidney failure or epilepsy, for example, then either humans must be experimented on or there can be no research at all. Is urgent human need more important than animal rights?

▼ **Do you agree with Peter Singer? Can you think of any arguments against his view? If you can, note them down.**

Some say that if we accept that it is right to experiment on animals in order to benefit millions of humans, then it might be right (and logical) to experiment on human beings for the same reason. This reasoning led to humans being experimented on by the Nazis and Japanese during the Second World War:

Is there any possibility of obtaining from you two or three professional criminals to be placed at our disposal? These tests, in the course of which the 'guinea-pigs' may die, would be carried out under supervision. They are absolutely indispensable to research into high-altitude flying and cannot be carried out, as has been so far attempted, on monkeys, whose reactions are completely different.
    [Letter from Dr Sigmund Rasher to Himmler, Nazi head of the Gestapo, 1944]

▼ **Some think that if we use animals for research we will soon use human beings. We might use criminals or people who need protection in our society. What is your opinion? Note down your view.**

Alternatives

Some people say that not all experiments on animals are useful or accurate, but the alternative does not have to mean experimenting on humans. Research goes on into alternative ways and to reduce the number of animals used.

❝ We should not base our view of the future on whether or not animal experiments have been useful in the past, but rather on whether they should be considered the most appropriate way of continuing biomedical research in the future. We must channel more resources into the development of reliable alternatives.

[Jacqueline Southee of FRAME]

FRAME (Fund for the Replacement of Animals in Medical Experiments) is an animal welfare charity that believes too many animals are used unnecessarily for live experiments. They do not see how the use of animals can be banned immediately, since animal experiments have evolved to play an important role in advancing medical knowledge, but this is their *eventual* aim. They are developing alternative methods that can replace animal experiments safely without restricting scientific progress.

▼ **Choose *one* of the quotations which you feel strongly about. What are your reasons for choosing it? Discuss your choice with a partner and listen to their view. Then, in groups of four, introduce your partner's choice and the reasons for it to the others.**

▼ **In groups discuss whether you think experiments on animals are a good or a bad thing. Afterwards write an individual account of your discussion.**

RELIGIONS

Abortion and Medical Ethics: Religions

Most religions rely on texts written many centuries ago, before some of these ethical problems were discussed. So there is often no clear guidance in their scriptures as to what one should do. Sometimes one can turn to declarations and statements made by conferences and gatherings of a particular religion. These can have official authority – such as the General Synod. Others are more informal, such as the Declarations made at the Assisi meeting. Remember that people have their own views too. So although a person may be a member of a religion, they may go against the religion's teaching in this area but still regard themselves as a member of the religion.

⊕ Buddhism

Abortion and medical technology

In Buddhist teaching there are five 'precepts' (or principles) which all Buddhists should try to keep:

1 To keep from harming others.
2 To keep from taking what is not given.
3 To keep from wrong sexual conduct.
4 To keep from lying.
5 To keep from alcohol and drugs because they cloud the mind.

There is in Buddhism no infallible authority, whether human or divine, whose opinion a person has to accept.

 The relevant precept would be the first, the personal undertaking to do no harm to any living thing, with the implied and understood requirement to develop a genuine attitude of loving-kindness and compassion to all.

[The General Secretary: The Buddhist Society]

So regarding transplants, for example, it would be for the individual to decide. Abortion, however, is a more complicated question. But again it would be for the individual Buddhist to decide what to do in the light of his or her decisions and actions.

 Although abortion appears to, perhaps really does, abrogate [break] the first principle, it might on balance, and in particular circumstances, yet be considered a necessity for compassionate reasons.

[The General Secretary: The Buddhist Society]

▼ **Buddhism seeks to do no harm to any living thing. How would you match that with the 'particular circumstances' the General Secretary mentions? Write down what you think those circumstances might be.**

Animals

Buddhist teaching is against killing. An important part of Buddhist teaching is that all creatures are in some sense 'one'. Buddhism teaches a doctrine of harmlessness which embraces all living beings.

 The Buddha in his time successfully preached against the then barbarous practices of wholesale animal sacrifice, pointing out that these were pointless, ineffectual in achieving their aim of influencing the gods, brutal and brutalising . . . A Buddhist worthy of the name would do all in his or her power to eliminate cruelty and suffering in its various forms and to protect all living beings.

[The Buddhist Society]

 Creatures without feet have my love,
And likewise those that have two feet,
And those that have four feet I love,
And those, too, that have many feet.

May those without feet harm me not,
And those with two feet cause no hurt;
May those with four feet harm me not,
Nor those who many feet possess.

Let creatures, all, all things that live,
All beings of whatever kind,
See nothing that will bode them ill!
May naught of evil come to them!   [Culla-Vagga v.6]

The fact that [animals] may be incapable of communicating their feelings is no more an indication of apathy or insensibility to suffering or happiness than in the case of a person whose faculty of speech is impaired. . . .

There is a striking similarity between exterminating the life of a wild animal for fun and terminating the life of an innocent fellow human being at the whim of a more capable and powerful person. . . .

[Buddhism is a] system which propagates the theory of rebirth and life after death, it maintains that in the continuous birth and rebirth of sentient beings (not only on this planet but in the universe as a whole) each being is related to us ourselves, just as our own parents are related to us in this life. . . .

We regard our survival as an undeniable right. As co-inhabitants of this planet, other species too have this right for survival. And since human beings as well as other non-human sentient beings depend upon the environment as the ultimate source of life and wellbeing, let us share the conviction that the conservation of the environment, the restoration of the imbalance caused by our negligence in the past, be implemented with courage and determination.

[The Buddhist Declaration on Nature]

▼   **The three verses from the Culla-Vagga show a great concern for animals. There are campaigns to 'Save the Whale' and stop the killing of baby seals. Do you feel the same about *all* animals? In a group discuss why you think people stress saving some animals rather than others.**

RELIGIONS

RELIGIONS

† Christianity

Abortion and medical technology

 Life must be protected with the utmost care from the moment of conception; abortion and infanticide are abominable crimes.

Christians believe that the world is created by God. Therefore all beings in the world come from God in one form or another. Human beings have a responsibility to care for all life, for everything in the world.

The Roman Catholic Church, together with the Orthodox Churches, forbids abortion *totally* – as we can see from the quotation above. In the *Declaration on Procured Abortion* (1974), the Roman Catholic Church also states:

 From the time the ovum is fertilised, a new life is begun which is neither that of the father nor of the mother. It is the life of a new human being with its own growth. It would never become human if it were not human already.

The Church of England and most Protestant Churches agree with the Roman Catholic Church *in principle*, but generally they accept that each case is special. Therefore while abortion should not be accepted – certainly *not* as a method of birth control – it may be permitted in certain cases:

1 if there is a serious risk to the mother's life
2 if conception takes place as a result of rape
3 if there is a grave risk that the baby will be born handicapped.

 We affirm that every human life, created in the divine image, is unique ... and that this holds for each of us, born or yet to be born. We therefore believe that abortion is an evil . . . and that abortion on demand would be a very great evil. But we also believe that to withhold compassion is evil, and in circumstances of extreme distress or need, a very great evil. . . . Christians need to face frankly the fact that in an imperfect world the 'right' choice is sometimes the acceptance of the lesser of two evils. [General Synod of the Church of England]

Paid surrogacy is rejected by Christians, though some Churches have been less firm about condemning in vitro fertilisation. In fact the views on experimentation and surrogacy in the Churches are similar to their views on abortion.

Euthanasia

Most Christian Churches oppose euthanasia. This is because of the command in the Bible not to take life. God created life, God will take it away.

▼ **What does it mean to say 'God created life, God will take it away'? Discuss in a group what you think the statement means.**

On the other hand, Dr Leslie Weatherhead, a Methodist preacher wrote:

 I sincerely believe that those who come after us will wonder why on earth we kept a human being alive against his own will, when all the dignity, beauty and meaning

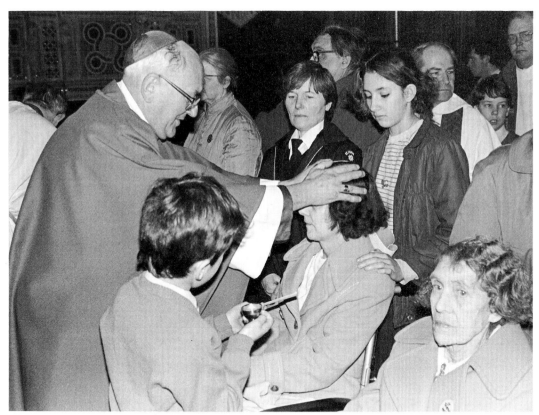

Spiritual healing is practised in many Christian churches. Here the Roman Catholic sacrament of anointing the sick with oil is being administered in Westminster Cathedral, London. Do you think spiritual matters are important in helping the sick?

of life had vanished . . . and when we would have been punished by the State if we had kept an animal alive in similar physical conditions.

Animals

> In the end, a lack of regard for the life and well-being of an animal must bring with it a lowering of man's self-respect, and it is [important] to our Christian faith that this world is God's world and that man is the trustee and steward of God's creation.
> [Dr Robert Runcie, former Archbishop of Canterbury]

▼ **Read again the statement by Dr Weatherhead. Write down why you think he says humans are allowed to live in a state in which we would put animals to sleep. Do you think we should treat animals and humans in the same way?**

▼ **Keep a look-out in any newspapers or magazines you read for items on the issues discussed in this chapter. Why do you think Christians should be specially concerned about them?**

▼ **Find out more about Christian medical ethics, e.g. from the Christian Medical Fellowship, and about the hospice movement, e.g. from The Information Officer, St Christopher's Hospice. (The addresses are at the back of this book.)**

 Hinduism

Abortion and medical technology

> His Being is the source of all being, the seed of all things that in this life have their life . . . He is God, hidden in all beings, their inmost soul who is in all. He watches the works of creation, lives in all things, watches all things.
>
> [Svetasvatara Upanishad]

This passage shows the reverence Hindus will have for *all* life. In the round of birth, death and rebirth, some Hindus believe one might be reborn as an animal, or even a tree or a stone. So all life is precious, God is the source of all things.

> In Him all things exist, from Him all things originate. He has become all. He exists on every side. He is truly the all.   [Mahabharata Shanti Parva 47–56]

Abortion would not be acceptable, though it is likely that in cases where the health of the mother is at risk it would be permitted. Hinduism, it should be remembered, does not have a central authority, so whether an abortion is permitted or not would depend upon the couple involved and the advice they might receive from a priest or friend.

Opinions are divided on artificial insemination as they are amongst most people. Men are reluctant to donate sperm, but an infertile couple might consider AID (see page 56) if the donor were a Hindu.

Euthanasia

A fundamental teaching in Hinduism is 'Perform your dharma' (obligatory duties). It is the basis of Hindu morality. Old age is to be respected.

> Let your mother be a god to you. Let your father be a god to you . . .
>
> [Taittiriya Upanishad 1.11.2]

Every householder is to care for those within the house. Death may come but it is only a stage on the path to the next rebirth.

> As a goldsmith, taking a piece of gold, reduces it to another newer and more beautiful form, just so this soul, striking down this body and dispelling its ignorance, makes for itself another newer and more beautiful form.
>
> [Brihadaranyaka Upanishad]

▼   **If death is only a step to another life, is it more likely to be easily accepted? What does your class believe about any future life? Does what they believe affect their thoughts or actions now?**

One of the most popular of Hindu gods is Ganesha (right). He has the head of an elephant and is thought of as the god of wisdom and the remover of obstacles. People pray to him at the beginning of any new enterprise. Do you think the Hindus' worship of Ganesha shows anything of their attitude to animals? Do you know of any other gods with animal features?

RELIGIONS

RELIGIONS

RELIGIONS

Animals

As you will realise from the above, Hinduism recognises God as being present in all things. So God is present in animals as well as humans. There is no clear difference between them. In some Hindu stories Ganesha (the elephant-headed god), Hanuman (the monkey god), Nandi (the bull on which Shiva rides), all have a major part to play – and there are many others. Vishnu comes down to earth (an avatar) in the form of different animals. So there is a strong link between the human and the animal world.

> **"** He who hates no creature, who is friendly and compassionate to all . . . he My devotee is dear to me. [Bhagavad Gita 12:3–14]

> **"** All creatures born from you, move round upon you. You carry all that has two legs, three or four. [Atharva Veda]

> **"** Turning to the animal world, we find that animals have always received special care and consideration. Numerous Hindu texts advise that all species should be treated as children. . . .
>
> The evolution of life on this planet is symbolised by a series of divine incarnations beginning with fish, moving through amphibious forms and mammals, and then on into human incarnations. This view clearly holds that man did not spring fully formed to dominate the lesser lifeforms, but rather evolved out of these forms itself, and is therefore integrally linked to the whole of creation.
>
> This leads necessarily to a reverence for animal life. The Yajurveda lays down that 'no person should kill animals helpful to all. Rather, by serving them, one should attain happiness.' . . .
>
> The Hindu tradition of reverence for nature and all forms of life, vegetable or animal, represents a powerful tradition . . .   [The Hindu Declaration on Nature]

Perhaps best known of all Hindu attitudes on this theme is their respect for the cow. Mahatma Gandhi said:

> **"** In its finer or spiritual sense, the term 'cow-protection' means the protection of every living creature.

The cow is an important symbol of the care which must exist between animals and all humans.

> **"** Everything in the universe, living creatures or rocks or waters, belongs to the Lord. You shall therefore only take what is really necessary for yourself, your quota. You should not take anything else, because you know to whom it really belongs.
> [Isa Upanishad]

▼   **Hindus believe God is hidden in all things. Why do you think that this belief is important to a Hindu's view of ethical issues? Discuss in a group what it might mean. Hindus believe in rebirth, so that might also be an important part of the discussion.**

▼   **Read again the quotation from the Isa Upanishad. Write down carefully what you think is necessary for yourself – your quota. Then write a few sentences about whether you could live only on your quota. To whom does everything else belong?**

 Islam

Abortion and medical technology

 Do not kill your children in fear of poverty. We shall provide for both them and you. Killing them is a big sin. [Qur'an 17:31]

Infanticide, abortion and other ways of getting rid of unwanted children are explicitly forbidden in the Qur'an, although it is recognised that having many children can be difficult. One passage from the Hadith says that:

 No severer of womb-relationship ties will ever enter paradise.

According to Sheikh Muhammad Mahdi Shamsuddin:

 Abortion is legal in one case only, and that is when the retention of the foetus or embryo in the uterus threatens the mother's life.

Dr Hassan Hathout believes, as a doctor and a Muslim, that there are two grounds for abortion:

 1 When there is certainty of danger in the immediate present or future to the mother's life or of serious harm to her health, or
2 When there is a strong or likely probability of the baby being born deformed or afflicted with a serious disease.

▼ **There seems to be a difference of opinion in the last two quotations about when abortion is permitted. Discuss these differences with a partner.**

Muslim men are forbidden from donating sperm to anyone other than their wives. It is felt that donating sperm to anyone else is equal to committing adultery.

Animals

A central part of Islamic teaching is that the entire universe is God's creation. God created the plants and the animals. While animal sacrifice is still carried out in Islam, the welfare of animals is of great concern.

 The Holy Prophet Muhammad was asked by his companions if kindness to animals was rewarded in the life hereafter. He replied, 'Yes, there is a meritorious reward for kindness to every living creature.'

All creatures on earth are conscious beings.

 There is not an animal on earth, nor a bird that flies on its wings – but they are communities like you. [Qur'an 6:38]

There are many Islamic laws forbidding vivisection. Ibn 'Umar reported that the Prophet condemned those who mutilated any part of an animal's body while it was alive.

▼ **Islam is very concerned about the welfare of animals. What is meant by the quotation from the Qur'an 6:38? Discuss what 'communities' means here and why the Qur'an should point out the 'community' spirit of animals and birds.**

✡ Judaism

Abortion and medical technology

There is a wide variety of views in Judaism. The rabbis (teachers) have given different views over the centuries. Certainly the Bible asserts that God created all things, but the issue of abortion is often concerned with *when* life exists in the womb.

> 66 When, in the course of a brawl, a man knocks against a pregnant woman so that she has a miscarriage but suffers no further hurt, then the offender must pay whatever fine the woman's husband demands after assessment. Wherever hurt is done, you shall give life for life . . . [Exodus 21:22–3]

This is taken to mean that the value of the life of the mother is greater than the life of the unborn child. The life of the unborn is valued by a fine, the life of the mother by another life. The foetus does not have the rights of a human being until it is halfway out of the birth canal.

It seems that, in Judaism, the *legal* bars to abortion are very few – on the other hand there is the moral dilemma.

> 66 Abortion is no substitute for birth control measures. It is appropriate when continuation of a pregnancy would harm the physical or mental health of the mother. The mother should be the primary person to decide what impairs her mental health . . . After 15 –17 weeks when foetal movements can be felt and it is apparent that the foetus is well developed, the claim of the foetus to human status becomes greatly strengthened.

▼ **The mother is considered important in questions of abortion; would you agree? Why is the mother so important? Read again Exodus 21:22 – 3, quoted above.**

Artificial insemination is permitted by rabbinic law as long as the donor is the husband. Artificial insemination by anyone else, as in Islam, is considered the same as adultery. The former Chief Rabbi, Lord Jakobovits, accepts the need for embryo research, as long as embryos are not created solely for research purposes.

He also states that organ transplants are allowed, as long as the probability of saving the patient's life is much greater than the risk to the donor. He lists some conditions regarding medical experiments:

1 Experiments may only be performed if they will benefit the patient.
2 Untried or uncertain cures may be used if safe treatment has failed to stop certain death.
3 In all other cases, it is wrong to volunteer for such experiments or force other people to take part.
4 If there is no serious risk to life and health, anyone may volunteer in order to help the health of others.

(*right*) *Adam and Eve in Paradise by Jan Breughel and Rubens. In paradise, Adam and Eve (representing the human race) are living happily in harmony with the rest of Creation. Eating the forbidden fruit is the symbol of human sin which brought evil consequences. Do you think human beings live in harmony with animals?*

R E L I G I O N S

Euthanasia

Euthanasia, in the sense of giving a patient a lethal dose, would not be permitted. However, Rabbi Moses Isserles stated:

 If there is anything which causes a hindrance to the departure of the soul . . . then it is permissible to remove it.

This might mean that the removal of feeding tubes and life-support machines would seem consistent with Jewish tradition. But not all Jews would agree with this.

▼ **Find out more about Jewish medical ethics, e.g. by writing to one of the addresses under 'Judaism' at the book of this book.**

Animals

 All of them depend on you [God]
to give them food when they need it.
You give it to them, and they eat it;
you provide food, and they are satisfied. [Psalm 104:27 – 8]

The Jewish tradition is one of harmony with the natural world. Although the Bible refers to animal sacrifice, they stopped this practice when the Temple was destroyed in 70 CE.

 'And the name that Adam gave to each living being has remained its name' forever (Genesis 2:19). In the Kabbalistic [Jewish mystic] teaching, as Adam named all of God's creatures, he helped define their essence. Adam swore to live in harmony with those whom he had named. Thus, at the very beginning of time, man accepted responsibility before God for all of creation.

[The Jewish Declaration on Nature]

 # Sikhism

The teachings of the Sikh Gurus (their spiritual teachers) do not contain any moral commands such as the Ten Commandments in Judaism and Christianity. The Sikh's ethical code arises out of a few simple, important ideas:

1 To love God's name.
2 To desire union with God.
3 God is the creator of all.

 'God is the destroyer, preserver and creator,
God is the Goddess too.
Words to describe are hard to find,
I would venture if I know.'
This alone my teacher taught,
There is but one Lord of all creation,
Forget Him not.   [Japji 5]

 Air, water and earth,
Of these are we made.
Air like the Guru's word gives the breath of life
To the babe born to the great mother earth
Sired by the waters.
The day and night our nurses be
That watch us in our infancy.
In their laps we play.
The world is our playground,
Our acts right and wrong at Your court shall come to judgement,
Some be seated near Your seat, some ever kept distant.   [Japji – the Epilogue]

These two short passages show that life, for the true Sikh, has real meaning in the search for God. Life has a purpose and is to be enjoyed.

Abortion and medical technology

Abortion is strongly disapproved of . It might only be considered if an unmarried woman became pregnant. However, like many other faiths, abortion would be acceptable if the life of the mother was at risk. There is no reason why Sikhs should not participate in conception by means of artificial insemination as long as the donor was the husband.

 I don't think there are any passages in the Guru Granth Sahib touching these subjects, particularly because they were not well known or an order of the day, especially heart transplants. The Sikhs these days would normally follow the general trend of society and are liberal and broadminded, excepting the very orthodox element. [Dr Chhatwal, Secretary, Sikh Cultural Society of Great Britain]

Animals

As we have seen, the Sikhs believe that God created the world. The passages above show that Sikhs believe they should care for the world and the creatures in it.

▼ General assignments

▼ **Think back over this chapter and briefly discuss in small groups whether all the religions seen to have something definite and clear-cut to say about all the ethical issues raised. Think about issues like abortion, artificial insemination, organ transplants. Discuss whether you would prefer to know exactly what you should and should not do, or whether you would prefer a more general moral guideline that left it up to you to decide.**

A Christian wrote:

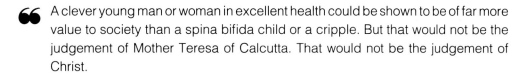 A clever young man or woman in excellent health could be shown to be of far more value to society than a spina bifida child or a cripple. But that would not be the judgement of Mother Teresa of Calcutta. That would not be the judgement of Christ.

▼ **Prepare a class statement in which you present clearly the arguments of the religions which support the idea of the value of all people, regardless of ability or physical or mental condition.**

Read the following quotation:

One should treat animals such as deer, camels, asses, monkeys, mice, snakes, birds and flies exactly like one's own child. How little difference there actually is between children and these innocent animals.

▼ **Having studied the section on Vivisection and Animal Rights, say whether you agree with this quotation. Then look back at the religions' views on animals and say which religion you think this quotation might come from.**

▼ **Apart from vivisection, there are other animal issues under constant debate, such as the slaughter of animals, culling (i.e. killing in order to control numbers), and conditions of battery hens and calves. Find out about an animal issue that interests you and give a short talk to your class about it.**

▼ **Of all the issues looked at in this chapter, choose the one that has interested you most. Find out more about it. There are books and addresses at the back of this book to help you. Collect your information in a folder and make an exciting project.**

▼ **Collect newspaper stories that are about some of the issues in this chapter. Read the stories carefully and present the opinions in them clearly. Give *your* opinion on the stories and the supporting arguments.**

RELIGIONS

3 The Natural World

▼ Introduction

This chapter is about the way human beings make use of the earth and its resources. Some of the words we often hear when people talk about this are **ecology**, **green**, **environment**, **pollution** and **radiation**.

Ecology deals with the way in which all living things depend on each other and their surroundings – the **environment**. We are becoming more aware of how much everything is linked together, and how human deeds can affect other creatures. Because the word ecology looks difficult, many people use the word **green**. Green is the commonest colour in nature. People concerned about 'green' issues are concerned about protecting nature.

One of the ways in which nature is threatened is through **pollution** of the atmosphere or the soil, rivers or the sea, with chemicals, smoke and gases, sewage and waste. A special type of hidden pollution can be caused by **radiation** from radioactive material. This is related to either the use of nuclear power stations, or the development of nuclear weapons.

This chapter looks at three issues: the greenhouse effect, the destruction of the rainforests and acid rain.

▼ **Discuss what effect it might have had on the astronauts to have seen the earth as it is in the photograph.**

▼ **In small groups share your feelings about the earth:**
What sort of things in the natural world do you find particularly beautiful?
What do you think is the relationship between human beings and animals?
Do you think the world exists for human beings especially?
Does it make sense to talk about a *purpose* in Creation? That is, was it made for some special reason even if we cannot always see it?

▼ **In the same or a different group discuss:**
In what ways do you think our environment is being spoiled? Write down what the group thinks are the four most serious problems.
Get a copy of a recent newspaper. Find a story about the environment, green issues or pollution, which might affect your area. What do you think should be done about it? Write a letter to a newspaper, on behalf of all of you.

▼ **When you have studied this chapter write down how you would sum up your attitude to the earth and its resources. You could do this in a piece of prose or poetry or, if the means are available, in a painting or piece of music.**

This is a satellite image of the earth, showing the continents of North and South America.
About thirty years ago such a picture would have been impossible

▼ The greenhouse effect

A hundred years ago it was thought that all the gas pushed out into the air by factories and coal fires was simply spread out and 'lost' somewhere. To some extent this is true. The earth can absorb a great deal of the carbon dioxide (CO_2) released into the atmosphere. It goes into the oceans and is 'used' by trees and other plants, in the process of photosynthesis, to produce oxygen. Above a certain level, however, the carbon dioxide simply collects in the atmosphere.

Temperature

It is important to understand that the earth is wrapped in a blanket of gases, of which at the moment 0.035% is carbon dioxide. These gases have what has come to be called a 'greenhouse' effect. The gases let sunlight through to warm the earth, just as glass lets sunlight through into a greenhouse. Some of the sunlight and heat is absorbed. A dark surface, such as the oceans, bare rock or the dark green colour of tropical forests, will absorb heat. The rest of the sunlight will be reflected – by light colours such as deserts and snow. But some of this reflected light does not pass back through the blanket of gases, or the greenhouse glass, because it is of a longer wavelength. It stays inside our atmosphere, and so raises the temperature.

The content of this blanket of gases has been held in balance for hundreds of thousands of years. The atmosphere lets out a certain amount of sunlight, and so keeps the earth at the same temperature. If too much heat was held in it would be unbearably hot. If too much heat escaped it would be unbearably cold. The living things on earth also affect this balance. The temperature of the earth without any life would be much hotter – about 290°C.

Industry

Since the huge increase in industrial activity over the last century and a half, the levels of carbon dioxide and other gases in our atmosphere have increased. It is also increased by motor vehicles and the burning of fuel for heating. It is estimated that the level of carbon dioxide in the atmosphere will double in less than a century. The blanket of gases is becoming thicker and so more of the sun's heat is being held in.

The rainforests

Other activities are also contributing to the build-up of greenhouse gases. The destruction of the rainforests throughout the world produces a lot more carbon dioxide into the atmosphere, as well as other gases such as nitrogen oxides. The trees are removed by the 'slash and burn' method. In 1978 80,000 square kilometres were cleared in Brazil alone. That is an area the size of Austria. In 1987 this had increased to 200,000 square kilometres of forest.

▼ **Ask your teacher how you can find out more about carbon dioxide and photosynthesis, or about CO_2 on other planets such as Mars and Venus. Write a summary of your findings.**

Greenhouse effect

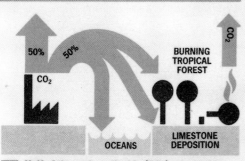

50% 50%
CO₂
BURNING TROPICAL FOREST
CO₂
OCEANS
LIMESTONE DEPOSITION

Half of the carbon dioxide (CO_2) released by industrial societies is absorbed by natural CO_2 "sinks" such as oceans, forests and the process of limestone deposition. The rest collects in the atmosphere.

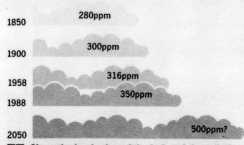

1850 — 280ppm
1900 — 300ppm
1958 — 316ppm
1988 — 350ppm
2050 — 500ppm?

Since the beginning of the industrial revolution CO_2 levels have been on the increase. Today the rate of increase is itself increasing, which could lead to a doubling of the 1850 level by the end of the next century.

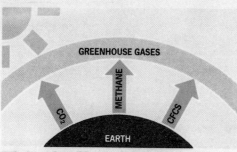

GREENHOUSE GASES
METHANE
CO₂
CFCS
EARTH

Apart from CO_2, atmospheric levels of methane and chloroflourocarbons (CFCs) are also on the increase. All three are greenhouse gases, warming the atmosphere by trapping the heat radiated back into it from the Earth's surface.

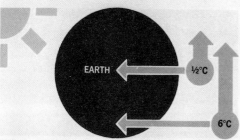

EARTH
½°C
6°C

By 2050 it is estimated that the atmospheric temperature could have risen by as much as 2°C. This average increase would be unevenly distributed, ranging from perhaps less than a degree at the equator to up to six degrees at higher latitudes.

CFCs and methane

Two other important 'greenhouse' gases are methane and CFCs – chlorofluorocarbons. CFCs are said to be 10,000 times more potent than carbon dioxide. They are also responsible for making holes in the ozone layer. They were used in aerosol spray cans, but a campaign against this has almost succeeded in stopping this practice. However, they are also used in refrigerators, air conditioning and some plastics, including food packaging – such as egg boxes and hamburger cartons.

Methane is said to be 10 times more powerful than carbon dioxide. It is produced by a wide variety of things – such as rice paddies, cows and rubbish tips.

▼ Find out about the Friends of the Earth or Greenpeace compaigns about CFC gases and write a short report as if you were writing an article for a newspaper.

▼ What is the ozone layer and why is it important? How did we become aware that it was being destroyed? Research into this, on your own or in a small group, and illustrate what you have found out, perhaps on a poster.

Temperature rises

The effect of such a huge increase of greenhouse gases in the atmosphere will cause a rise in the average air temperature on earth of 2–3°C. This does not sound a very large increase in temperature, but remember that this is an average increase, and it will not be evenly distributed. The increase will cause ice in the polar regions to melt and the sea level to rise. Much low-lying land will be flooded. Not all the effects can be predicted, but there is enough evidence to sound a loud warning about the need to think hard about the consequences of our way of life.

▼ Try to work out the effects on Britain if the world warms up. What parts would flood first? What would be the effect on crops? Can you think of other effects? If possible, check your findings from expert sources.

▼ The rainforests

Why are rainforests so important? Here are some reasons:

They produce oxygen

The true tropical rainforests are like a girdle around the earth, along the equator. They represent half the world's forests. One third of the world's biological activity takes place in them. The biologist Harald Sioli calculated in 1971 that the Amazon Basin, through photosynthesis, produces approximately 50% of the oxygen added to the earth's atmosphere annually, and consumes about 10% of the carbon dioxide in the atmosphere.

They regulate the world's climate

Tropical forests are extremely important for the world's climate. In higher latitudes we depend on tropical forests to keep us warmer, through the circulation of water vapour. Also, the enormous quantities of water vapour produced help to cool the tropics on both sides of the equator.

The Wasusu tribe in the Amazon. Their way of life and their continued existence is threatened by the destruction of the rainforest. Look at a map of South America and find the Amazon rainforest

The Amazon rainforest

They preserve different species

It is estimated that over half the world's species are found in the rainforests. The rate of extinction of species due to human interference may be many hundred times greater than in any recent period. The consequences of this are still not even worked out.

They yield a variety of products

Tropical trees produce resin for paints, oils for flavouring and perfumes, vanilla and cocoa for food, brazil nuts, rubber and, in particular, ingredients for many medicines and drugs. If trees are destroyed, future cures for some illnesses might be lost for ever.

▼ **Write a summary of what might happen if the rainforests were destroyed. Discuss your ideas with one or two people before you begin.**

Why are the rainforests being destroyed?

The forests are being cleared for immediate economic reasons. The countries concerned are usually poor, and many have huge debts to repay. They want to develop their industries and earn more money from abroad through timber, beef or mining. In countries like Brazil where there is a very large, poor population, they want to provide land and jobs for the people. Action has been taken without thinking about the longer-term consequences.

Logging

Tropical hardwood trees, like teak and mahogany, are cut down and sold abroad, to be made into things like doorframes and tables. In many countries there are few controls and the trees are cut carelessly, damaging other trees, plants and wildlife. Too many trees are cut down and little replanting is done. The demand for hardwood is especially difficult because hardwood trees take a much longer time to grow than softwood. Even when the good intention is there, it is virtually impossible to replace these trees at the rate they are consumed.

Forests into cattle ranches

Another way of making money from abroad is by exporting beef:

 During the third quarter of this century alone, the area of man-made pastureland in Central America more than doubled, almost all at the expense of tropical forests. The same applies to South America; between 1966 and 1978 some 31,000 square miles of Brazil's Amazonian jungle – an area equal in size to Austria – were cleared for 336 cattle ranchers, and another 20,000 ranches of varying sizes were also established. The government's goal was to make Brazil the world's leading beef exporter by the early 1980s. Brazil remained a net *importer* of beef because the pasturelands were not as fertile as had been expected.

The quality of the soil under the rainforests is very poor. So more and more land is needed for the cattle to graze. It also means that they produce inferior meat, which is only fit for use in hamburgers. This is why hamburgers are cheap.

 The price of a US hamburger does not reflect total costs, and especially environmental costs, of its production in Latin America.

Other reasons for destruction

The rainforests are also cleared for roads and railways, for fuel production (such as charcoal) and for mineral extraction (such as gold and iron ore). In Papua New Guinea trees are felled, whole hillsides at a time, to provide newsprint and packaging wood-chips for Japan.

Hydroelectric dams flood huge areas of a forest, destroying the wildlife and tribal people's lands. They provide cheap electricity for towns and industries. In Brazil, settlers move into the forests. Most have few farming skills. They clear the land by cutting down or setting fire to the trees. But the soil is not good for growing crops, so many of these settlers move on, to clear yet more forest.

Consequences of destruction

You were asked on page 83 to write down some of the things which would happen if the rainforests were destroyed. Here are three more effects which have not been mentioned so far.

Soil erosion

Forests retain large quantities of rain water. Rainforests, in particular, protect the poor soil from the ravages of the sun and the force of the rain. When the trees are destroyed, there is frequently massive erosion of the soil and the creation of rock-hard, useless land. In Panama, it has the added effect of washing large quantities of silt into the rivers, and eventually into the Panama Canal. This has caused difficulties in navigation, because the dredging of the canal is unable to keep pace. Elsewhere, the destruction of forests causes landslides which can obliterate roads.

Floods

A most serious effect which many in Bangladesh and elsewhere have already experienced is devastating floods, caused once again by deforestation. There is also a threat to supplies of drinking water. This is because, after forests are felled, water runs off the mountains more rapidly, and little water soaks into the ground to replenish springs and streams.

Destruction of tribal life

In Central and South America, Malaysia and other countries around the world, the destruction of the forest also destroys the home environment and livelihood of many tribal peoples. Many are made homeless. Some die because of pollution of their rivers and the introduction of diseases they are not protected against.

▼ **Do you think that simple tribal life can be preserved? What are the difficulties? What do you think should be done? Share your ideas in a small group.**

▼ **When it is said that the world must stop destroying the rainforests, the reply is sometimes made that it is important to provide a living for poor people who have no other work and not enough to eat. Arrange carefully a class debate on the subject.**

▼ **Take one aspect of this topic of the rainforests and look into it further. This can be done on your own or in groups of two or three. (There are some books and addresses listed at the back of this book.) You could illustrate it for display or gather your information in a loose-leaf book. Here are some ideas, you can probably think of others:**
   1 The problem of deforestation in a particular country, e.g. Brazil, Panama, Bangladesh (because of the removal of forests in the Himalayas), Malaysia, Ghana.
   2 Tropical rainforests and climate. How does the warm, moist air of the rainforests affect the climate in the rest of the world?
   3 The rare species of life in rainforests. Choose about five of these to study and report about.

▼ Acid rain

Factories, power stations and motor vehicles belch out a vast number of gases. Some of this falls near to its source; the rest combines with water vapour in the air to make acids, which may end up in rainwater. This is called 'acid rain'. Acid rain poisons lakes and rivers, the soil, plants and trees, especially those which are long-lived and are therefore given doses over a long period of time. It also damages buildings.

The two most poisonous gases are sulphur dioxide – which when mixed with water vapour turns into sulphuric acid, and nitrogen oxides – which become nitric acid. Most of the nitrogen dioxide (NO_2) comes from motor exhausts and power stations. About 73% of sulphur dioxide in the UK also comes from power stations.

▼ **Calculate the emission of nitrogen dioxide *per person* in each country. For example, the emission per person in France is 1,297,000 ÷ 55,279,000 = 0.02 tonnes. Five countries have the same quantity per person. Which are they? Place the other five countries in rank order. Write a brief comment on your findings.**

	NO_2 (tonnes per year)	Population
USA	21,510,000	239,283,000
E. GERMANY	1,895,000	16,644,000
UK	1,888,000	59,972,700
CANADA	1,704,000	25,309,330
FRANCE	1,297,000	55,279,000
NETHERLANDS	401,000	14,615,000
BELGIUM	290,000	9,858,895
SWEDEN	247,000	8,358,139
DENMARK	181,000	5,124,794
NORWAY	102,000	4,198,637
1987 emissions of NO_2 from various countries		

In 1987 Norway experienced some rain so acid it could have been lemon juice. Rain as acid as vinegar has fallen in Kane, Pennsylvania, and rain almost like battery acid was once measured in Wheeling, West Virginia.

An international problem

Before the 1960s, smoke from factories affected mostly the areas near to them. In an attempt to improve conditions, it was thought that it would be better to spread the waste gases as widely as possible. It was believed that they would be 'diluted' harmlessly in the atmosphere. So the height of the chimneys was increased. This was a serious miscalculation and instead of making the pollutants disappear, they were simply spread over a wider area to produce an international problem of acid rain.

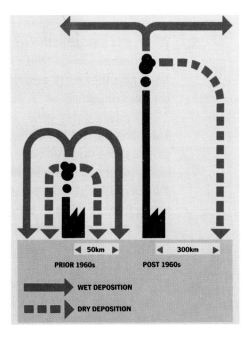

50km PRIOR 1960s 300km POST 1960s

WET DEPOSITION
DRY DEPOSITION

What are the effects of acid rain?

1 The acid 'leaches' out of the leaves the nutrients trees need for growth, such as potassium, calcium and magnesium.
2 It attacks the nutrients in the soil. So trees cannot make up the loss from their leaves by taking up more with their roots.
3 It brings in concentrations of aluminium and cadmium into soil and water, which attack and kill the root systems of plants and trees and kill fish and other wildlife. Sweden's 20,000 lakes are acidified and 4,000 of them no longer have any fish.
4 It eats away at buildings. Some ancient buildings have been more damaged in the last 20 years than in the last 2,000 years.

▼ **Cars produce many of the harmful gases which cause this pollution. Environmental groups (such as the World Wide Fund for Nature) say that people must use cars less and fewer roads should be built. Cars must be less polluting and use fuel more efficiently, *now*. Do you think the government should *force* people to do these things? What about people's *freedom* to drive when and where they want? Write a short newspaper article exploring this topic. Consider the consequences for car manufacturers, people's freedom and mobility, as well as the pollution issue.**

A site in the Harz mountains, Germany in 1970   *The same site in 1985. What happened in between?*   ▼

Are there any solutions?

In recent years there has been an increasing awareness of the damage to the environment. We have become conscious, too, that the world's resources are limited and that the peoples of the world depend on each other. One country's industrial growth is another's acid rain.

▼ **In pairs write down what solutions you think should be explored to reduce global warming. This means looking for ways of putting less of the 'greenhouse' gases into the atmosphere and ways of taking up more of the CO_2 which is released. Think carefully about the effect of any particular solution. Do this before going on.**

Personal decisions

Perhaps the solutions we think of last of all are the things that we and our families can do. For example, we could try to use less energy by switching off unnecessary lights, use public transport instead of going by car, buy environmentally friendly products, plant more trees, and so on. You can probably think of others. People tend to blame governments and industry for the problems caused to the environment. But governments might say they do what people want them to do, industries might say that they provide what people want.

❝ Living is polluting. Our very presence on the planet makes us all exploiters of its natural wealth and contributors to the vast volume of waste we collectively spew out into earth, air and sea. In essence, *we* have created today's ecological crisis, not industry or government. After all, it is we who demand industry's products and continue to condone the government's environmentally damaging policies. This is why the notion of individual responsibility is central to the business of cleaning up the planet and developing sustainable ways of creating wealth in the future. It's down to each and every one of us to do our bit for the future by learning to tread more lightly on the planet *right now*. [Jonathon Porritt, former Director of Friends of the Earth]

▼ **Do you think that 'tread more lightly on the planet' is a good expression? Write a paragraph in your own words to say what it means.**

Alternative sources of energy

Another solution is the development of alternative sources of energy, ones which do not cause the emission of carbon dioxide and other gases. These alternative sources include wind and water power, wave power and sun power – solar energy. Wind power is well-established around the world but in Britain it is considered experimental. Britain does, however, lead the world in making wave-power generators, and has thousands of water wheels that are no longer used which could be restored. Some people believe the potential is there. Those who support alternative energy say that all that is needed is support from the government.

Rows of panels containing solar cells. This power station in California is capable of transforming the sun's radiation into electrical energy. One problem is that it takes up a lot of space

The further development of nuclear power has also been suggested as a solution, though this brings with it yet other dangers of pollution.

Political and economic problems

All nations try to create and protect their own wealth, and protect their own people. Unless nations can co-operate, it will be difficult to find solutions. There is a need to persuade people about the seriousness of the present situation.

Take the destruction of the rainforests. Solutions must consider the economic and political aspects. The economic part is concerned with how the large numbers of poor people in these countries are going to make a living. How can we say that logging, mining, and dams for electricity should be stopped, if we don't offer another way for the poor people of these countries to earn a living?

Some of these countries have huge international debts. Developing countries owe rich countries over 1,300 billion dollars. Will the rich countries get the political co-operation of developing countries by saying that, because we have now found out that industry causes too much pollution, you must not have industries, or clear your rainforests, to pay off your debts?

▼ **This chapter cannot cover the whole field of environmental concerns or the possible solutions. However, with the help of your teacher and other departments in your school such as the science department, you may wish to investigate other solutions to some of these problems, or look at different problems, such as the threat to wildlife or the oceans, the use of pesticides and fertilisers, radiation, nuclear waste and nuclear accidents such as Chernobyl, hydro-electric dams such as the Aswan Dam, etc. Remember to look at all sides of the topic.**

The Natural World: Religions

▼ The Assisi Declarations

> 66 We, members of major world religions and traditions, and men and women of good will, are gathered here, in this marvellous Church of St Francis, to awaken all people to their historical responsibility for the welfare of Planet Earth, our Sister and Mother, who in her generous sovereignty feeds us and all her creatures.

These are the words of Father Lanfranco Serrini, Minister General of the Order of St Francis. He was speaking at a huge gathering of members of many different faiths and members of many conservation organisations on 29 September 1986. It was the 25th anniversary of the World Wide Fund for Nature International. The place was the Basilica of St Francis in Assisi, Italy. St Francis is sometimes called by Christians 'the patron saint of ecology', or the 'green saint', because of his great love of nature and his feeling of being *part* of it. In his poetry he referred to Brother Sun and Brother Wind, Sister Water and Mother Earth.

Many important religious leaders took part in the event to declare where they stood on conservation. Out of this grew the new Network on Conservation and Religion – a programme of action, reflection and education.

▼ **Find out more about the life of St Francis. Illustrate the most important events in his life and write down whether you think 'patron saint of ecology' is a good title for him and why or why not.**

▼ **Find out more about the Network on Conservation and Religion, from the World Wide Fund for Nature UK (the address is at the end of this book). Prepare a report for the class.**

▼ **Ask your teacher to obtain *The Assisi Declarations* from the World Wide Fund for Nature UK (the address is at the end of this book). Organise a reading followed by group discussion.**

Every religion has a view about the natural world. What a religion says about the natural world, and the place of human beings in it, is a very important part of what a religion is about.

(right) A modern painting of St Francis of Assisi. Look carefully at it and describe what you see. What do you think the artist is trying to say about St Francis?

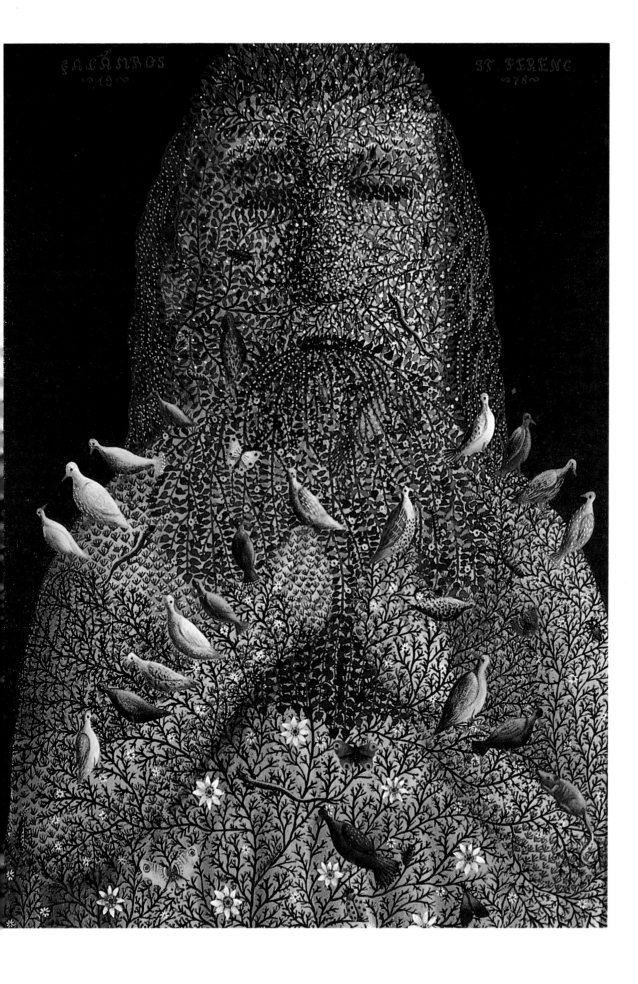

RELIGIONS

⊕ Buddhism

No doctrine of creation

Traditional Buddhist teaching has no teaching about how the world was created. There is no teaching about a creator god. The Buddha's teaching is concerned only with those things which will help the follower to get to Nirvana.

Cause and effect

Here are three paragraphs from the Declaration at Assisi made by the Buddhists:

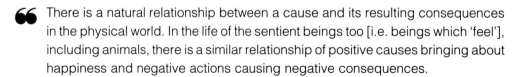

66 There is a natural relationship between a cause and its resulting consequences in the physical world. In the life of the sentient beings too [i.e. beings which 'feel'], including animals, there is a similar relationship of positive causes bringing about happiness and negative actions causing negative consequences.

This is a very important part of Buddhist thinking. It says that thoughts and actions make things happen. Not only that, but good thoughts and good actions make good things happen.

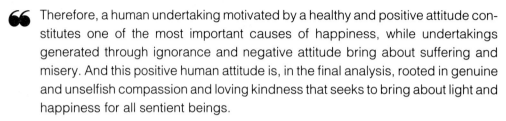

66 Therefore, a human undertaking motivated by a healthy and positive attitude constitutes one of the most important causes of happiness, while undertakings generated through ignorance and negative attitude bring about suffering and misery. And this positive human attitude is, in the final analysis, rooted in genuine and unselfish compassion and loving kindness that seeks to bring about light and happiness for all sentient beings.

Here the writer is saying that people ought to influence the state of things around them. If they take a positive and helpful attitude in anything, it contributes to the happy outcome of the project. While if people are nasty and selfish it brings nothing but misery.

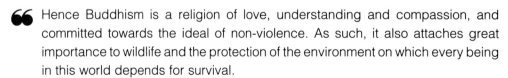

66 Hence Buddhism is a religion of love, understanding and compassion, and committed towards the ideal of non-violence. As such, it also attaches great importance to wildlife and the protection of the environment on which every being in this world depends for survival.

▼ **Discuss Buddhist thinking about cause and effect. Do you think that thoughts make things happen? Or just actions? Do you think *everything* we do is important? What about words? Does it matter what we *say*? Buddhists believe there is no escape from the consequences of an action. Try to make up a story starting from just one happening. Everything in the story must follow from the result of a previous action.**

Harmlessness and compassion

In Buddhism it is not so much 'obedience to laws' which is important, but what kind of behaviour helps people to understand things better and helps them to escape from the 'suffering' of the world. 'Suffering' here means the unsatisfactory nature of life and the world because they do not last. Keeping certain rules (precepts) just clears the path a bit. The principle of 'harmlessness' (ahimsa; see page 131) is usually thought of as not harming other humans, but it extends to animals and all living things in general.

RELIGIONS

May creatures all abound
in weal and peace; may all
be blessed with peace always;
all creatures
weak or strong,
all creatures great and small;
creatures unseen or seen,
dwelling afar or near,
born or awaiting birth,
– may all be blessed with peace!

Just as with her own life
a mother shields from hurt
her own, her only, child, –
let all embracing thoughts
for all that lives be thine,
– an all-embracing love
for all the universe
in all its heights and depths
and breadth, unstinted love,
unmarred by hate within,
not rousing enmity.

[Sutta Nipata]

Living in harmony with nature

There is in Buddhism the feeling that human beings are *part of* the natural world in which they live, and they should not be trying to force change upon it. Rather we should seek to live in harmony with it. One would expect Buddhists to be particularly concerned to preserve the natural things on earth. However, countries with large Buddhist populations have mostly been caught up in the need to compete in modern industrial processes.

▼ **What difficulties are there in following Buddhist principles in the world today? Discuss this in small groups and write down some ideas. (Two difficulties might be that in order to live in the modern world we need large resources of fuel and raw materials, and that competition between nations leads to the build-up of huge defence systems.)**

The photograph shows Buddhist monks at Chithurst Forest Monastery in West Sussex engaged in a project of conservation. One activity involves carefully thinning some woodland to allow other species of tree to have enough light to grow. Another involves planting a meadow with wild flowers almost extinguished by agriculture. Are there projects near you that you could become involved in?

RELIGIONS

✝ Christianity

A divine Creator

Christians believe in a divine Creator and that the earth therefore has a divine purpose. They see Jesus Christ as the agent of all creation.

> I believe in one God
> the Father Almighty,
> Maker of heaven and earth,
> And of all things visible and invisible:
> And in one Lord Jesus Christ,
> the only-begotten Son of God,
> Begotten of his Father before all worlds,
> God of God, Light of Light,
> Very God of very God,
> Begotten, not made,
> Being of one substance with the Father,
> *By whom all things were made.*   [Part of the Nicene Creed]

God is in the world

> He [Jesus Christ] is the image of the invisible God, the first-born of all creation; for in him all things were created, in heaven and on earth, visible and invisible, whether thrones or dominions or principalities or authorities – all things were created through him and for him. He is before all things, and *in him all things hold together.*   [Colossians 1:15–17]

Pilgrims of different faiths at the twenty-fifth anniversary of the World Wide Fund at Assisi, Italy in 1986. The picture has many symbols. How many can you find?

RELIGIONS

A stained-glass window by Marc Chagall in Chichester Cathedral. It illustrates Psalm 150. The last verse reads: 'Let everything that has breath praise the Lord: O praise the Lord.' Look up the psalm in a Bible and try to match the words to the picture

RELIGIONS

RELIGIONS

Christians not only believe that God created the world, but also that in the coming of Jesus Christ, God is in a special way *in* the world. That 'in him all things hold together'.

▼ **Discuss the meaning of this last phrase as used in Colossians (page 94). What difference do you think it ought to make to Christians? Write a few sentences to summarise your conclusions.**

Dual citizenship

Christianity teaches that human beings become citizens of both heaven and earth. On earth they have a stewardship of God's creation. That is, they have been given the job of looking after it. Human acts which harm creation are an offence against God the Creator.

 So then you are no longer strangers and sojourners, but you are fellow citizens with the saints and members of the household of God.   [Ephesians 2:19]

Speaking for all of nature

In Christian teaching there is also another idea. The whole of creation, together with human beings, is included in a great plan by God – which is impossible for us to visualise. In the meantime, human beings are to *speak* for all creation. It is the special gift of human beings to be able to speak and express themselves and Christians have the responsibility of speaking for all of nature.

▼ **Do you think that the sense of being the 'spokesperson' for nature would make a difference to a person's attitude?**

In a very ancient hymn, various parts of nature are invited to turn to praise God. Here is part of it:

 Bless the Lord all created things:
   sing his praise and exalt him for ever . . .
Bless the Lord sun and moon:
   bless the Lord you stars of heaven;
bless the Lord all rain and dew:
   sing his praise and exalt him for ever.
Bless the Lord all winds that blow:
   bless the Lord you fire and heat;
bless the Lord scorching wind and bitter cold:
   sing his praise and exalt him for ever.

▼ **Write down 10 ways in which human beings have interfered with the natural world. Pick out those ways which have been beneficial and those which have been harmful. Are there some things which have been *both* beneficial and harmful? How should a Christian try to improve things?**

▼ **Try to write a hymn about nature which has the same style as the one quoted above.**

 # Hinduism

The Hindu Declaration on Nature at Assisi included the following passages:

The human race is not separate from nature

 In the ancient spiritual traditions, man was looked upon as part of nature . . . This is very much marked in the Hindu tradition, probably the oldest living religious tradition in the world. . . .

Hinduism believes in the all-encompassing sovereignty of the divine, manifesting itself in a graded scale of evolution. The human race, though at the top of the evolutionary pyramid at present, is not seen as something apart from the earth and its multitudinous lifeforms.

This means there is God at the top, then lesser gods and other spiritual beings, then human beings then animals and so on. But they are all wrapped together in one.

Nature is sacred

 The Hindu viewpoint on nature . . . is permeated by a reverence for life, and an awareness that the great forces of nature – the earth, the sky, the air, the water and fire – as well as various orders of life including plants and trees, forests and animals, are all bound to each other within the great rhythms of nature. The divine is not exterior to creation, but expresses itself through natural phenomena . . . .

Apart from this, the natural environment also received the close attention of the ancient Hindu scriptures. Forests and groves were considered sacred, and flowering trees received special reverence. Just as various animals were associated with gods and goddesses, different trees and plants were also associated in the Hindu pantheon [the complete group of divine beings]. The Mahabharata [a Hindu sacred book] says that *even if there is only one tree full of flowers and fruits in a village, that place becomes worthy of worship and respect.'* Various trees, fruits and plants have special significance in Hindu rituals.

The earth is our mother

 This earth, so touchingly looked upon in the Hindu view as the Universal Mother, has nurtured mankind up from the slime of the primeval ocean for billions of years. Let us declare our determination to halt the present slide towards destruction, to rediscover the ancient tradition of reverence for all life and, even at this late hour, to reverse the suicidal course upon which we have embarked. Let us recall the ancient Hindu dictum: '*The earth is our mother, and we are all her children.'*

▼ **List the three main attitudes towards the earth described in the Hindu declaration. What difference can you notice between the Hindu and the Christian view?**

The following quotation is from the scriptures called the Upanishads. It expresses the Hindu view which feels that the ultimate cause of the universe (Brahman), the earth and the individual human being, are not really separate. (The word, or the 'sound', OM, represents for Hindus the ultimate or the divine and almost always comes before a prayer or an important statement.)

66 OM. In the centre of the castle of Brahman, our own body, there is a small shrine in the form of a lotus-flower, and within can be found a small space. We should find who dwells there and we should want to know him.

And if anyone asks, 'Who is he who dwells in a small shrine in the form of a lotus-flower in the centre of the castle of Brahman? Whom shall we want to find and know?'

We can answer: 'The little space within the heart is as great as this vast universe. The heavens and the earth are there, and the sun, and the moon, and the stars; fire and lightning and winds are there; and all that now is and all that is not: *for the whole universe is in Him and He dwells within our heart.*'

[Chandogya Upanishad: VIII, i, 1–3]

This is how OM (or AUM) looks written down. It is not only the sound which is important. The visual symbol itself is used very frequently as a focus of meditation. It represents the sense of the last line of the quotation from the Chandogya Upanishad

Form small groups and discuss the meaning of the passage quoted above. (It is summed up in the last phrase.) How might it affect the way we feel about nature? With the help of your teacher, bring together the findings from the whole class into just three statements.

▼ **Find out more about the symbol OM and the symbol of the lotus-flower and prepare a visual display.**

 # Islam

The greatness of God

The most important statements in Islam are about Allah (God). In the following two surahs (chapters from the Qur'an) God's greatness is described – how He knows all things and how what we know is by His will.

Islam forbids the use of images of God or of human beings. For this reason Islamic art has developed very strongly in decoration and calligraphy (artistic writing). The word here is 'Allah' in Arabic

RELIGIONS

RELIGIONS

66 God, there is no god but He, the Living, the Everlasting. Slumber seizes him not, neither sleep; to Him belongs all that is in the heavens and the earth. Who is there that shall intercede with Him save by his leave? He knows what lies before them and what is after them, and they comprehend not anything of His knowledge save such as he wills. His throne comprises the heavens and the earth; the preserving of them oppresses Him not; He is the All-high, the All-glorious. [2:256–7]

66 It is He who stretched out the earth and set therein firm mountains and rivers, and of every fruit He placed there two kinds, covering the day with the night. [13:5]

Creation has a purpose

These words from the Qur'an say that human beings have minds which can tell them that God's creation has a purpose provided their attitude is one of praise to Allah.

66 Behold! In the creation of the heavens and the earth, and the alternation of night and day – there are indeed signs for men of understanding – Men who celebrate the praise of Allah, standing, sitting, and lying down on their sides, and contemplate the (wonders of) creation in the heavens and the earth, (with the thought): 'Our Lord! not for naught hast Thou created (all) this! Glory to Thee! Give us salvation from the penalty of Fire.' [2:30-3]

Trustees of God

66 For the Muslim, mankind's role on earth is that of a 'khalifa', viceregent or trustee of God. We are God's stewards and agents on earth. We are not masters of this earth; it does not belong to us to do what we wish. It belongs to God and He has entrusted us with its safekeeping. Our function as viceregents, 'khalifa' of God, is only to oversee the trust. The 'khalifa' is answerable for his/her actions, for the way in which he/she uses or abuses the trust of God . . . .

His trustees are responsible for *maintaining the unity of His creation, the integrity of the earth*, its flora and fauna, its wildlife and natural environment.
[The Muslim Declaration on Nature]

▼ **Try to write down another way of saying what is meant in the words in italics in the passage above.**

66 So unity, trusteeship and accountability, that is 'tawheed', 'khalifa' and 'akhrah', the three central concepts of Islam, are also the pillars of the environmental ethics of Islam. [The Muslim Declaration on Nature]

▼ **Learn the three Arabic words for unity, trusteeship and accountability.**

▼ **Study carefully once again the Hindu and Islamic views of nature. In what important aspects do they differ? Discuss and then prepare a short piece of writing showing how the different approaches might affect behaviour towards the environment, if at all.**

✡ Judaism

The creation of the world by God

The best-known account is the story of the seven days of creation in Genesis:

 Then God said, 'Let us make man in our image, after our likeness; and let them have dominion over the fish of the sea, and over the birds of the air, and over the cattle, and over all the earth, and over every creeping thing that creeps upon the earth.' So God created man in his own image, in the image of God he created him; male and female he created them. And God blessed them, and God said to them, 'Be fruitful and multiply, and fill the earth and subdue it; and have dominion over the fish of the sea and over the birds of the air and over every living thing that moves upon the earth.' And God said 'Behold, I have given you every plant yielding seed which is upon the face of all the earth, and every tree with seed in its fruit; you shall have them for food. And to every beast of the earth, and to every bird of the air, and to everything that creeps on the earth, everything that has the breath of life, I have given every green plant for food.' And it was so. And God saw everything that he had made, and behold, it was very good. And there was evening and there was morning, a sixth day.   [Genesis 1:26–31]

A world created for man

 There is a tension at the centre of the Biblical tradition, embedded in the very story of creation itself, over the question of power and stewardship. The world was created because God willed it, but why did He will it? Judaism has maintained, in all of its versions, that this world is the arena that God created for man, half beast and half angel, to prove that he could behave as a moral being . . . . man was given dominion over nature, but he was commanded to behave towards the rest of creation with justice and compassion. Man lives, always, in tension between his power and the limits set by conscience.   [The Jewish Declaration on Nature]

We are in the boat together

 Some twenty centuries ago they told the story of two men who were out on the water in a rowboat. Suddenly, one of them started to saw under his feet. He maintained that it was his right to do whatever he wished with the place which belonged to him. The other answered him that they were in the rowboat together: the hole that he was making would sink both of them.

We have a responsibility to life, to defend it everywhere, not only against our own sins but also against those of others. We are all passengers together in this same fragile and glorious world. Let us safeguard our rowboat – and let us row together.
                    [The Jewish Declaration on Nature]

▼   **In small groups, consider the lesson of the small rowboat. Make a list of occasions when people have claimed the right to do what they like with their own place or their own life and when you would like to say 'we are in the rowboat together'. Then try to make up a similar story which would help to show people that their actions affect more than themselves.**

RELIGIONS

 Sikhism

The world as the sphere of dharma

> God created the night, the seasons, days of the month and week.
> He created the wind, water, fire and the worlds below.
> In their midst He set the world as the sphere of dharma.
> In it He placed animals of various species and colour,
> Their names are many and endless.
> Each one is judged according to his deeds.
> The Lord Himself is True and His Court is true,
> There the elect rejoice in their acceptance.
> They bear the sign of grace and mercy.
> There the bad and good are separated . . . .
>
> In the stage of Truth, the Formless One resides.
> He, the Creator, beholds His creation and looks upon it with grace.
> Here there are continents, worlds and universes.
> Who can describe a boundless bound?
> Here there are worlds within worlds and endless forms.
> Whatever God wills that they do freely.
> God beholds creation and rejoices.   [Japji 34, 37]

Dharma is a Sanskrit word and it means a number of things in English – *law and duty* when one is referring to individuals, *order and structure* when referring to Creation. In the passage above, Guru Nanak says that the world is the 'sphere of dharma' and he means that God created the world as the place where each species, including humans, has to live out its destiny and follow the inner law (dharma) of its being. They will subsequently be judged in God's 'court'.

The earth's custodians

The idea of human beings as custodians of God's creation follows naturally as part of their dharma. However, Sikhism inherits the Indian tradition of the indwelling of God in all things. He is the 'Formless One'.

> The heaven is thy salver, the sun and moon thy lamps,
> The stars in their paths are thy scattered pearls.
> The fragrance of sandalwood is thine incense,
> The wind is thy chowri and all the forests thy flowers, Lord of Light!
> What worship this is! This is thy worship, Destroyer of rebirth!
> The unstruck Word is thy temple drums.
>
> Thousands are thine eyes, yet thou hast no eye.
> Thousands are thine images, yet thou hast no form.
> Thousands are thy pure feet, yet thou hast no foot.
> Thousands are thy fragrances, yet thou hast no fragrance.
>   [Rag Dhanasri, Adi Granth]

The Sikhs' Holy Book is a collection of hymns by the Gurus and other saints. Guru Gobind Singh was the tenth Guru and he said that after him this book should be their Guru. So it is called the Guru Granth Sahib. It is treated with great honour and respect as would be paid to a living leader. While the book is open there is always an attendant. The 'chauri', a fan which is a symbol of authority, is waved over it from time to time

▼ **General assignments**

We can look at the natural world in different ways. We might have, for example, a religious, humanist or scientific outlook. We are also influenced by economic pressures and our own developed personal feelings.

Even if we do not belong to any religion there is still an influence at 'second hand' because religions affect the culture of the country in which we are brought up.

▼ **Consider each of the religious attitudes you have studied and write down anything which you feel is common to them all.**

▼ **Christianity, Islam, Judaism and Sikhism all have the idea that human beings are God's *stewards* (Christianity) or *trustees* (Islam) or *viceregents* (Judaism). Discuss whether you think this is a good way to think about our responsibilities. Can you find any differences in emphasis between the religions? Does it possibly make human beings too arrogant?**

There is in some countries a strongly developed 'humanist' tradition. Humanists do not

believe in God, but believe that it is important to behave in a loving way towards one another and to protect the planet from destruction. Many would argue that they are the allies of the scientists and take an objective but caring view of the world.

Those people who look at the earth in an objective, scientific way see the earth as a huge resource for human beings to use to their own advantage. If problems result, science will find a solution.

66 The evidence of all history is that science and technology have been giving us a progressively better life rather than a progressively poorer life in all kinds of material ways . . . That is, science and technology have been giving us longer life, better health, richer lives, more resources, a cleaner environment – all the material goods of life, and there's no reason why they should not continue to do that for ever.   [Professor Julian Simon, co-author of *The Resourceful Earth*]

▼   **Form small groups, and using your experience from previous assignments, sort out your views about Professor Simon's claim.**

Do you think it is right to take direct action which is dangerous and may be against the law?

Peace and Conflict

European arsenals to be cut

Pakistan fears Indian attack over Kashmir

▼ Introduction

These newspaper headlines are fairly typical of the daily news brought to us each day. They show that we live in a troubled world. We see conflict in wars between nations and civil wars between different groups within the same country. There is conflict between political parties and mistrust between people of different cultures. Even next-door neighbours can get involved in mini-battles! When we think about our own lives and the people around us we can probably find other examples of conflict.

▼ **In small groups discuss the following questions:**
What types of conflict have been left out from the list above (e.g. conflict between different generations)?
What are some of the main causes of conflict between: friends, relations, neighbours, different cultures, nations? Write down at least two causes under each heading.

▼ **What items in the news recently show examples of conflict? Using newspapers and magazines make a collage of headlines of your own choice. Try to give examples of domestic, local, national and international conflict.**

▼ **Are there any ways in which conflict can be healthy and useful? For example, does conflict help us to make important choices about right and wrong, good and evil?**

▼ **Find out some examples in the news of people trying to build up peace. If you can, make another collage to go with the one on conflict. Why do you think television, radio and newspapers give more time and space to conflict than to peace?**

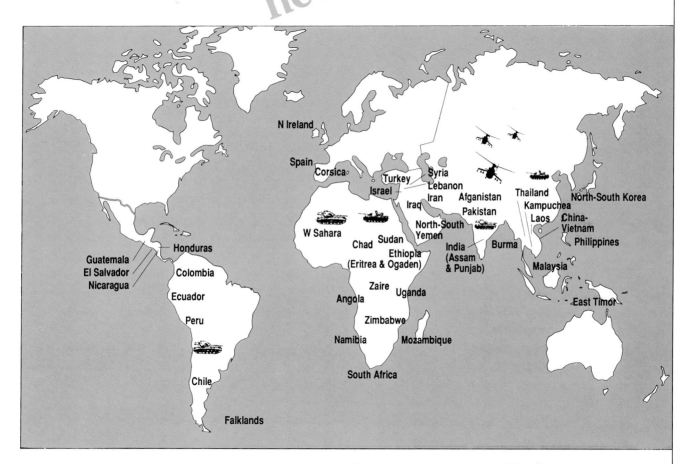

Look at this map, which shows the military conflicts going on in the world in 1984. Choose two of these conflicts and find out:

1 which countries were/are involved
2 the main causes of the conflict
3 whether the USA or USSR were/are involved

▼ **Collect newspaper and magazine articles and pictures on military conflicts or wars which are taking place at the present time and with the help of others make a wall display with short captions which will tell the reader precisely what the situation is.**

The Falklands War

66 For me and many of my colleagues, as we went down to the South Atlantic, the war was a distant dream. It was our duty to go. We were sailing south in the belief that it was only fair and right to protect the freedom of British subjects. If we didn't stand by them in their hour of need, we would be failing them. If we believed in freedom ourselves, we had no choice.

This is what Simon Weston of the Welsh Guards wrote about the Falklands War which took place between Britain and Argentina in 1982.

The Falkland Islands were given their name by a British sailor, who was the first to land in 1690. Small groups of British people lived there on and off until Argentina set up a colony in 1826. They were expelled by the British in 1833, and since then the islands have been continuously lived on by British people. In 1982 there were only 1,600 people on the islands, but the British Government felt it had a duty to protect their rights since the islanders wanted to remain British citizens. International law also states that people have the right to say who should govern them.

Within three days of the Argentine invasion, a huge Task Force set sail for the South Atlantic to recapture the islands. Within two months the war was over. Over a thousand men were killed in the fighting. Many more were wounded and maimed. The war cost Britain at least £2 billion.

 66 We all felt an enormous sense of relief. My main feeling was that no more young men were going to have to die. It was not like winning a football match or anything like that. There was just an enormous sense of relief that it was over and that we could all go home. [Brigadier Julian Thompson of the Royal Marines, speaking about the surrender]

▼ **With the help of an atlas find the Falkland Islands. How far are they from Britain (approximately)? Argentina claims the Malvinas (the Argentine name for the Falklands) are Argentine territory. Do you think they have good reasons for this? Discuss in a group whether it is important to know which nation owns the territory.**

▼ **Do you think the British Government should have sent the Task Force? Are you able to reach some form of agreement in your groups?**

Key events in the war

2.4.82	Argentina invaded Falklands
5.4.82	British Task Force set sail
25.4.82	Island of South Georgia recaptured
1.5.82	Special Air Service (SAS) and Special Boat Squadron (SBS) land on the Falklands. Also first bombing raid on Port Stanley
2.5.82	Argentine cruiser *General Belgrano* sunk with the loss of 368 lives
4.5.82	HMS *Sheffield* sunk
21.5.82	British forces landed at San Carlos. HMS *Ardent* sunk
23.5.82	HMS *Antelope* sunk
25.5.82	HMS *Coventry* and *Atlantic Conveyor* sunk
28.5.82	Battle of Goose Green
8.6.82	Disaster at Fitzroy: 51 killed (mainly Welsh Guards) when ships *Sir Galahad* and *Sir Tristram* were bombed
11.6.82	Battle for hills above Port Stanley began
14.6.82	Argentina surrendered at Port Stanley

For and against

Many books have been written about the Falklands War by soldiers, journalists and politicians. Many express opinions about whether or not Britain should have sent the Task Force to recapture the islands. Some say that it was a waste of life and of money to fight over a group of islands 8,000 miles from Britain. Others argue that there was a principle at stake, that the islanders themselves should decide which country governs them. Here are two different ideas about the Falklands War:

66 The whole affair is one of tragedy. War is a messy, dirty, miserable business and we should never ever allow ourselves to go to war.

[A British soldier who fought in the Falklands]

66 We went to fight because they invaded British territory and it's really all a question of pride. I think Britain had to have that pride in herself . . . They had to do it. Oh, the price that my family paid! No one will ever know. . . . Perhaps it was worth it for Britain's sake. [A woman whose husband was killed in the war]

▼ **You may wish to read more about the Falklands War yourselves. You should find a selection of interesting material in your local public libraries.**

▼ **In small groups discuss some of the following statements:**
'It was our duty to go.'
'If we believed in freedom ourselves, we had no choice.'
'We should never allow ourselves to go to war.'
'The whole affair is one of tragedy.'
'Perhaps it was worth it for Britain's sake.'

May 1982. The British Task Force leaves Portsmouth for the Falklands. What are your reactions to this picture?

Voices from the battlefield

It is difficult to imagine what it is like to be involved in a real battle. Here are some experiences of soldiers during the Falklands War. For most of these men, it was their first taste of being on the battlefield.

The battle for Goose Green

 It's dark, there's an enormous amount of noise, there's incoming fire to you, there's white phosphorous going off to provide smoke, there's tracer coming towards you and going away from you. There's fear running through you. You close up towards trenches, you throw grenades, you fire your weapon, you bayonet. It's savage gutter fighting. Everything you've ever experienced before is nothing like it. It is basic killing.

A member of the Scots Guards

 You can always tell when you're close to someone when they've been hit because you hear the crack of the bullet and then you hear a terrible sort of 'thwack' – it's sort of solid flesh and bone and it's an extraordinary noise – very grim.

One of our soldiers had a night sight and suddenly saw one of them. We heard the crack and we heard the thud when it hit the Argentinian. There was a moment's silence and then the most terrible screaming: he was screaming for his mother. There was complete silence from both sides as both of us listened to it. I'm sure we were just as horrified as the Argentinians. It really was an awful noise. It went on and on and on.

A Royal Marine speaks about clearing up the bodies after a battle

 You would find a wallet on them with a picture of them with their wife and kids and I would look at it and think 'this could have been me lying there'.

Every body we came across was all twisted. You could see the agony these guys had been in when they died. Then we found an Argentinian officer who had been injured. He had a belly wound. He started talking to me in English and he was telling me he didn't know why we were fighting either.

I felt bad about the bodies and the state of them and everything. You know the way we would just toss them into a hole . . . They were just kids.

The guy who was injured . . . I just wish he'd never spoken English . . . he died.

After the assault on Tumbledown Mountain

 I didn't like the Argentinians, and I wouldn't admit to myself that they were the same as us; you can't, else you can't do warlike things to them. About an hour after the war had ended and we had finished taking out all the casualties, I felt drained. I also felt a deep resentment towards the Argentinians. Near us was a row of our lads who were dead, lying under a tarpaulin, with their feet sticking out. Young men – never to laugh again.

I was thinking of them when I was brought an Argentinian casualty who was obviously in great pain as he'd been very badly shot up. He was just an eighteen-

June 1982. British wounded arrive in Montevideo, Uruguay, after the British–Argentine conflict in the Falklands

year-old lad, of peasant stock. He looked bewildered and terribly afraid. He'd got big brown eyes – I shall never forget them, they were staring out like chapel hat pegs. He was obviously terrified that these British swines were going to do terrible things to him, but all we were going to do was take him straight away to a surgeon where he'd get exactly the same treatment as our boys.

He was well-strapped up, so Jay put him on a litter, but the noise of the helicopter rotors and all the rest of it must have really scared him. He was in a hell of a state, so Jay leaned over and pinched his cheek and gave it a gentle little shake and a pat. This lad's whole face lit up with relief and all the anger and resentment which I felt against him evaporated in an instant. It was great, because that purged my system completely. You can't allow yourself great humanitarian feelings when people are trying to kill you, but, when the battle is over, it's like after a boxing match – you're all friends together. And I felt like that; I felt like reaching out and touching this chap and reassuring him. But I couldn't because I was strapped in, so I looked over at him and gave him a big wink.

▼ **Why do you think the Royal Marine was upset by the Argentinian officer speaking English?**

▼ **Choose a phrase from one of these passages which interests or even shocks you. Explain to those in your group the reason for your choice.**

▼ **In small groups make a list of war films which:**
a) make war out to be romantic
b) try to give a more realistic picture of war.

▼ Hiroshima

On a bright sunny day on 6 August 1945 the United States dropped an atomic bomb on the Japanese city of Hiroshima. This was the first time a nuclear weapon was used. Three days later a similar bomb was dropped on Nagasaki. Japan then surrendered. Two hundred thousand people had been killed by the two bombs and thousands more were to die later from the effects of radiation. Below is an account from Takae Ishii a survivor from Hiroshima.

I was there . . .

 I was eighteen at the time and working in a naval establishment. That August morning I had taken leave to go and visit some relatives who had been evacuated to the country. I left home with my mother to go to the station in Hiroshima. An alarm was sounded and we feared it was a heavy American attack so we hurriedly returned home. We heaved a sigh of relief when the alarm was finally called off.

Hiroshima, August 1945

A huge firework display . . .

 Suddenly, on that splendid summer day, there was a tremendous flash and a moment later the whole sky burst into flames. It was like being in the middle of a huge firework display with crackling all around us and sparks flying all over the place. My mother threw herself on top of me and in that instant the house collapsed on us in a resounding crash. I don't know what happened afterwards. It was as if time stopped. . . .

Not a single house was still standing . . .

 Gradually we began to make out sounds coming from outside. We could hear weeping and shouting, the voices of people calling for their loved ones. Eventually we made our way through the fallen beams and the rubble out into the open where we saw the emptiness and desolation all around us. Not a single house was still standing, and the trees which just a short time before had been a mass of green foliage were reduced to ash. From the clouds of dust which surrounded us flames leapt up here and there. We thought it was dangerous to stay where we were and we decided to go to a large garden which belonged to the old nobility of Hiroshima. . . .

Naked bodies burnt to cinders . . .

 When we reached the garden it was unrecognisable, nothing was left of the towering trees but a few burnt stumps. It was crowded with refugees like ourselves and we were being sprinkled with a shower of ash which was coming from the fires on the opposite bank of the river. 'We must live,' repeated my mother. 'Pray to Buddha with all your strength.'

Night fell and the smoke from the fires, tinted an unnatural red by the flames, stretched like a funeral pall over one side of the sky. During the night the noise of the lamenting both near and far seemed to echo from the centre of the earth. The next morning we decided to walk to the house of a relative about three miles away. The city was a pile of rubble, and naked bodies burnt to cinders, littered the streets. I saw a woman who was trying to feed her dead baby and a child who was crying over the dead body of his mother. There were so many bodies strewn around it was impossible to avoid treading on them and they had already begun to decompose in the heat of the summer sun. We were absolutely exhausted but we managed to reach the ruins of our house just before nightfall. My father and my brother were searching the rubble for our bodies. We looked at each other and without uttering a word embraced, the silence broken only by our weeping.

The horror of war did not come to an end with the declaration of peace. First of all there was the mammoth task of burning all the bodies. The soldiers heaped them up until there was a pile as high as a two-storey building and the cremation lasted several days. Then there were the effects of radiation.

Soon the symptoms began to show . . .

 We went to live with some relatives and soon the symptoms began to show. My father developed a disease of the lungs of which he was eventually cured but his thick black hair began to fall out and his body became shrunken like that of an old man. My mother lost her sight and her hearing and I suffered from acute anaemia which immobilised me completely. But much more serious were the wounds to the spirit. Perhaps I had witnessed so much horror for one so young that I began to hate everyone, including myself. I saw everything in a negative light. Even when things began to rise again from the ashes I couldn't find any pleasure in life. I hated the world around me and at times I felt like putting an end to it all.

▼ **Discuss these questions in small groups:**
Why do you think the author wanted to 'put an end to it all'?
Many of the accounts written about this event mention that it was a bright summer's day. Why do you think they bother to tell us this?
What do you think the author means by 'the wounds of the spirit'?
What are your feelings after reading this passage? You may wish to express your feelings through poetry or painting or some other way. Discuss this with a friend before deciding.

'I was glad that they dropped the bomb'

The decision to drop the two atomic bombs was made by President Harry Truman and a dozen American and British advisers. It was felt that the war against Japan could drag on for a further 18 months and cost over a million Allied lives. The British people were weary after six years of war and the American forces had already paid heavily in lives in the war in the Pacific. Much of the United States' industrial power had been used up in war material. The dropping of the bombs was intended to frighten the Japanese into an immediate surrender. It succeeded in doing this.

The following statement is from an Englishman imprisoned by the Japanese during this time. He said:

66 I was glad that they dropped the bomb. I was a Japanese prisoner of war. The bomb saved me from a slow lingering death.

▼ **Do you think that the atomic bomb should have been dropped? Divide your page into two halves with two headings:**

Reasons for dropping the bomb   Reasons against

In your groups try to fill in reasons in each column and weigh up the arguments. What would you have advised the President if you had been consulted?

(right) Hiroshima, the fortieth anniversary. Look back at the photograph on page 112. Do you think it is a good idea to keep one building as a ruin? Why, or why not?

▼ Nuclear war

Since atomic bombs were dropped on Hiroshima and Nagasaki at the end of the Second World War, nuclear weapons have been created which are 50–100 times more powerful. It is estimated that there are about 60,000 nuclear weapons in the world today. Einstein, the famous physicist, once said:

> ❝ On the assumption that a Third World War must escalate to nuclear destruction, I can tell you that the Fourth World War will be fought with bows and arrows.

The arms race

Many people feel that we have lived under the constant threat of nuclear war for over 40 years. Over this period there has been a kind of deadly competition between the USA and USSR and their allies. Each side tried to beat the other in inventing more powerful nuclear weapons and in ways of delivering them. This could be, for example, from deep silos dug out in the desert of Nevada or from huge submarines cruising under water for months at a time. The USA even began a research programme into space weapons (SDI) which could destroy enemy missiles possibly with laser beams. It is sometimes referred to as 'Star Wars'. All this was very expensive. The world spends billions of dollars *every year* on weapons and armies.

The deterrent

Other people point out that this has been a small price to pay for keeping the peace. They feel that although we have not succeeded in preventing wars, there has been no major world-wide conflict since the Second World War. This is, they say, entirely due to the fear of nuclear weapons and their terrible destructive power. Those who advise that we should destroy all our nuclear weapons no matter what anyone else does are called 'unilateralists'. Those who think reductions in nuclear weapons can only take place when agreed by both sides are called 'multilateralists'.

The end of the cold war

In 1987 there was an agreement between President Reagan of the USA and President

Gorbachev of the USSR to destroy all their ground-based intermediate-range nuclear weapons. This represented 3% of their nuclear weapons. This was the first-ever treaty to actually *cut* the number of nuclear weapons rather than just to limit the numbers made. It also meant the destruction of a whole category of nuclear weapons.

Some of these American weapons were based in Britain. These were called 'cruise' missiles. They were all removed in 1989.

Further talks and agreements on arms reductions are taking place. Some politicians say that no matter how much we *reduce* the number of weapons, we must never get rid of the nuclear deterrent.

In recent years there have been quite sudden changes in the countries of Eastern Europe which were part of the bloc of countries allied with the USSR. There were peaceful revolutions in East Germany, Czechoslovakia, Hungary, Poland and Bulgaria, and violent revolution in Romania. In 1990 East Germany was reunited with West Germany.

President Gorbachev announced his desire to get rid of all nuclear weapons eventually. The need for vast defensive forces seems to be less pressing.

But Harold Macmillan, a former Prime Minister, said:

❝ If all this capacity for destruction is spread around the world in the hands of dictators, reactionaries, revolutionaries, madmen – then sooner or later . . . either by error or insanity, the great crime will be committed.

▼ **Discuss in small groups whether we should always keep a nuclear weapon 'deterrent' in this country or not.**
   a) **Do you think that what Macmillan said could happen?**
   b) **Do you think that giving up nuclear weapons would encourage others to do the same?**

Women watch at Greenham Common Airfield as a US Air Force transport plane loads cruise missiles to return them to the United States for dismantling – January 1989. Do you think the 'Greenham Common Women' could feel justified in their long protest?

▼ Justified violence?

The Just War

If you have ever seen films about life in the Middle Ages you will know that war was part of everyday life. Most towns were fortified to protect the inhabitants from invading armies. In the thirteenth century St Thomas Aquinas set down guidelines in an attempt to control the many wars that were taking place around him. This resulted in five conditions which must be met in order to justify going to war. Some Christian leaders continue to use these as guidelines when asked their view.

1 A war cannot be started by any individual person. It must have the authority of the State. In other words it must be *started and controlled by the sovereign or the government.*
2 There must be a *just cause* for going to war. In other words a wrong must have been committed like the seizing of land, and so on.
3 There must be a *right intention*, for example the removal of evil or to bring peace.
4 War must be the *last resort*. All other means to resolve the situation must be tried first.
5 There must be *proportionality* to the way war is fought. This means a nation should only use enough force to achieve its aims and no more. As far as possible the war should only involve casualties amongst soldiers and not civilians. If civilians are in danger of being killed, then there has to be a justifiable reason. The war must also be 'in proportion' to the original wrong committed.

▼ **People are divided on whether or not there can ever be such a thing as a 'Just War'. What do you think? In small groups discuss the issue. The following questions may help your discussion:**

   a) **What was the main reason for condition 1?**
   b) **Think of two examples of wars this century which you think agree with condition 2.**
   c) **Do the two examples you have chosen have a 'right intention' as laid down in condition 3?**
   d) **Is it possible to always comply with condition 4?**
   e) **Does condition 5 really protect civilians from the horrors of modern warfare?**
   f) **Is it possible to fight a war in a humane way and still win?**
   g) **Does the threat of nuclear war make any difference to our attitude towards the 'Just War' theory?**

Is political violence justified?

Someone who agonised over the whole issue of violence being used by Christians was Dietrich Bonhoeffer, a German Lutheran pastor. He lived during the rise of the National Socialist Party (Nazis) in Germany. He was so appalled by the evils of Nazism that he joined in the plot to assassinate Hitler. When questioned about this use of violence Bonhoeffer replied:

 If I saw a drunken driver racing down the street, I would not consider it my duty to bury the victims of the madman. It would be more important to wrench the wheel out of his hands.

Romanians placing candles for those killed during the fighting in Bucharest in December 1989. They were rebelling against a totalitarian regime. Do you think it is always justifiable to fight against unjust rulers? Can you think of any reasons why it might not be?

The attempts on Hitler's life failed. The conspirators were rounded up and executed. Bonhoeffer himself was hanged at Flossenburg concentration camp just four weeks before the end of the war in Europe.

▼ **In a library, look up more information on Bonhoeffer's life, especially on his last two years in prison, and make notes on his thoughts about the use of violence.**

▼ **Write an imaginary conversation between Dietrich Bonhoeffer and a religious person who finds it difficult to justify the use of violence. You may wish to perform your 'dialogue' in front of the class.**

▼

119

▼ Pacifists

How would you feel if war suddenly broke out and you were called to go and fight for your country? Would you be prepared to take up weapons and kill another human being? Would it depend upon who you were fighting and for what reason?

Conscientious objectors

Throughout history there have always been people who have refused to use violence. These people are known as *pacifists*, which basically means 'peace-makers'. In the case of war they have refused to fight for their nation, claiming to be conscientious objectors. Their conscience tells them to object when they are called up (conscripted) to the armed forces.

Cartoon from 1917. Some countries still put people in prison if they refuse to do their military service. Do you think this is a fair practice? Try to think of both sides of the argument

Conscientious objectors did not have an easy time and faced long periods in prison. Perhaps the worst part for them was the reaction of other civilians. They were labelled as cowards and traitors and they were made to feel as outcasts.

Letter from a conscientious objector

The following is an extract from a letter written by a conscientious objector during World War Two:

I registered as a CO on March 9th, 1940, and afterwards appeared before the local CO Tribunal in Leeds to which I had submitted the following statement in support of my application for complete exemption from military service:
  'I refuse to have anything to do with war because I believe that there is a latent goodness in every human being and consequently see no justification for killing men in ruthless warfare. These convictions have been strengthened by my acquaintance not only with Englishmen, but with Frenchmen, Germans and Czechs, and men of other nationalities. My religious conceptions lead me to think kindly towards everyone and teach me to banish hatred and prejudice from my mind. On these grounds I apply for complete exemption from military service.'

▼ **Discuss these questions in pairs:**
How would you feel if you were called up to fight?
Do you think conscientious objectors are cowards?
Would you be willing to go to prison for your beliefs?
In what circumstances, if any, would you be prepared to die for your beliefs?

Here is another letter. This was written to a CO from his girlfriend in 1939:

Quite frankly, I think you talk a lot of tripe, you might be a conscientious objector but it won't do you a bit of good. I know it isn't the least bit of good talking to you or even trying to change your opinions about war, but the fact remains that you as an individual cannot do one bit of good trying to stick to, what you consider to be, very high ideals about fighting . . . A little while ago you joined the Auxiliary Fire Service, you joined of your own free will . . . In joining the AFS you were releasing a man to go out and fight for his country, therefore you are as much to blame if that man kills an enemy as he is. You say you do not want to kill a man. Well, my dear, who does? No man on this earth **wants** to kill another. I admit it is a nasty thought, but if you would only use that dumb brain of yours and understand that men do **not** quite deliberately fight to kill, they fight to defend, which is an entirely different matter.

▼ **How would you feel if you were the CO who received this letter? Write a letter back defending your beliefs.**

▼ **Find out whether countries outside Britain make allowances for conscientious objectors.**
or
Find out as much as you can about the Peace Pledge Union or the pacifist beliefs of the Quakers (Society of Friends). (You will find addresses at the end of this book.)

Peace and Conflict: Religions

RELIGIONS *(vertical text in left margin)*

▼ Religions and war

Almost every day you will find newspaper reports of wars and conflict in which religion is involved.

> ▼ **Find a recent newspaper and find out how many of the reports about fighting are connected with religion.**

It is not possible to say which conflicts will be 'news' when you read this. At the time of writing, the conflict in Northern Ireland continues. This involves differences between Catholic and Protestant Christians. In Lebanon, Christian and Muslim militias fight each other, and both fight amongst themselves. Some Sikhs are trying to establish an independent state in Punjab in northern India and are in conflict with Hindus. Sinhalese Buddhists are in conflict with Hindu Tamils in Sri Lanka. Of course, it is not *only* religion that people are fighting about, but it is quite clear that religion is involved.

It is not only in the present day that religion has been involved in wars. Can you think of examples from history when religion has had an important part in war?

> ▼ **Some people think that there are things more important than living – things they would die for. The Crusaders in the Middle Ages were willing to give their lives to regain Christian control of the holy places in Palestine, for example. What is the most important thing for you? Would you risk your life for it?**

Religions are important

Why do religions seem to be so dangerous? It is because they are so important to people. Most people in the world live their lives in a religious context. Religions are systems which give meaning to people's lives. They also help people to organise themselves in families, groups and nations. So when people feel that their religion is threatened, they feel that they are losing everything. People from every religion come into contact much more often today and we have to find out how best to live together.

Religions and peace

Religions have been at the centre of some very unhappy events in the world in the way that they have engaged in violent conflict. Furthermore, people of all religions will justify violence in certain circumstances. This is true even of religions which have a great reputation for being tolerant and peaceful, such as Buddhism and Hinduism. Buddhist countries engage in military conflicts and consider such defensive activity permissible. Hinduism, although it has a pacifist element, considers it important to follow one's 'dharma'.

At the same time, religions have been the source of inspiration for almost all the greatest achievements of humanity.

The great religions are all well-tried ways of organising life in society to get a goal. That goal is described in different ways in each. All these goals have something to do with *peace* – the peace of heaven, the peace of release or moksha, the inner peace of Nirvana, the ultimate peace of union with God.

Religions in recent times have been the inspiration for many efforts towards peace in the world. In October 1986 there was a great gathering of religious leaders at Assisi in Italy. Representatives of Muslims, Hindus, Sikhs, Jains, Parsees, Buddhists, Shintoists, traditional African religions, American Indians, Jews and Christians, met to make a declaration together for peace.

▼ **Discuss these questions in small groups, and at the end write some notes about your discussion:**
Do you think Religious Education in schools could help to build peace between religions?
Do you think it is important for politicians and government leaders to understand the religions of the world?
What other kinds of things would help?

Under the word 'Peace' written in many languages sit (from left to right) the Archbishop of Canterbury, Dr Robert Runcie; the Archbishop of Thyateira and Great Britain, His Eminence Methodius; Pope John-Paul II, and the Dalai Lama. They gathered to pray for world peace at Assisi on 27 October 1986. How many of the languages can you identify?

Buddhism

Peace

The following passages are by Walpola Rahula, a well-known Buddhist monk from Sri Lanka. They show how Buddhists consider peace and human compassion as the most important aims for the world.

Self-discipline is better than military power

❝ Buddhism aims at creating a society where . . . one who conquers himself is more respected than those who conquer millions by military and economic warfare . . .

Goodness should conquer evil

❝ [a society where] hatred is conquered by kindness, and evil by goodness; enmity, jealousy, ill-will and greed do not infect men's minds . . .

Compassion is central

❝ [a society where] compassion is the driving force of action; where all, including the least of living things, are treated with fairness, consideration and love . . .

Nirvana is the goal

❝ [a society where] life in peace and harmony . . . is directed towards the highest and noblest aim, the realisation of the ultimate Truth, Nirvana.

Nirvana is the spiritual state which all Buddhists aim to achieve. The word itself means 'be extinguished' or 'blown out' – like the flame of a candle. It comes through 'enlightenment'. We have seen elsewhere (page 66) that the first of the Buddhist precepts or rules is to avoid harming others.

❝ Just as a mother would protect her only child even at risk of her own life, even so let one cultivate a boundless heart towards all beings.
Let one's thoughts of boundless love pervade the whole world – above below and across – without any obstruction, without any hatred, without any enmity.

This passage is from the Metta Sutta ('sutta' means 'sayings'). Metta is the Pali word for 'loving-kindness'.

The Dhammapada

The Dhammapada is one of the best-known books in Buddhist scriptures. The sayings are thought to be the words of the Buddha himself. Here are some passages about conflict and peace:

❝ Though one man conquer a thousand times a thousand men in battle, he who conquers himself is the greatest warrior.

❝ Better than sovereignty over the earth, better than the heaven-state, better than dominion over all the worlds is the first step on the noble path.

RELIGIONS

(The 'noble path' is the Noble Eightfold Path which leads in the end to Nirvana.)

4
PEACE
AND CONFLICT

66 Victory breeds hatred, for the conquered is unhappy. The calm one is he who has given up both victory and defeat.

66 All men fear pain and death, all men love life. Remembering that he is one of them, let a man neither strike nor kill.

66 Hatred does not cease by hatred; hatred ceases only by love. This is the eternal law.

▼ **In small groups discuss the statement: 'He who conquers himself is the greatest warrior.' In your discussion:**
   a) Make a list of the kind of things we all want.
   b) Think about whether it is useful to have control over our desires.
   c) Consider whether some desires are easier to control than others.

▼ **Write a few words on what you think is meant by 'The calm one is he who has given up both victory and defeat.'**

▼ **Find out about the 'Four Noble Truths' and the 'Noble Eightfold Path.' Do you think these teachings would help to bring about a more peaceful society?**

Buddhists have built peace pagodas, like this one in Battersea Park in London, throughout the world, to remind people how terrible war is. Sometimes peace gardens have been made instead. Find out if there is one near your school that you could visit

RELIGIONS

✝ Christianity

The Peace of Christ

Jesus said:

> 66 Peace I leave with you; my peace I give to you; not as the world gives do I give to you. [John 14:27]

Peace is very much at the heart of the teaching of Jesus, yet Christians have long been divided about whether it is ever right to go to war or use violence. And opinions are very

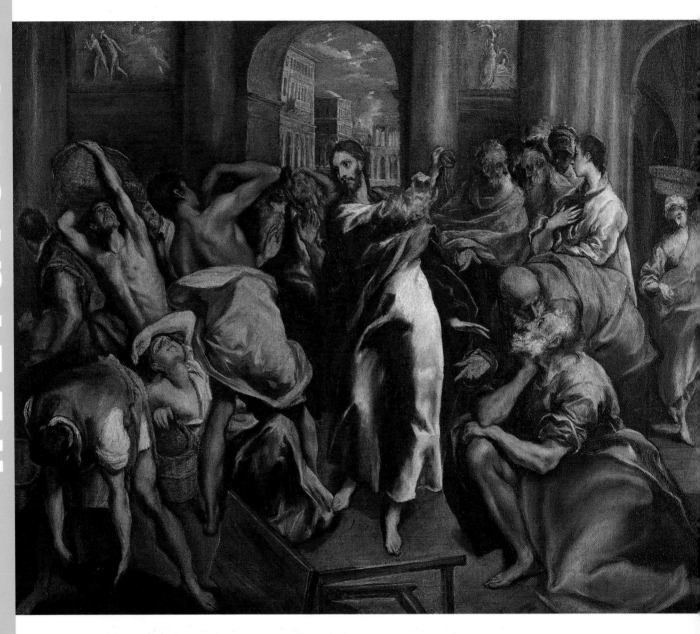

'Christ driving the money changers from the Temple' by El Greco. Read Mark 11:15–18. This incident is often quoted by people who argue that Jesus was not opposed to the use of violence when used against evil. Do you think it is a sound argument?

R E L I G I O N S

strongly held! They all believe that war is wrong, but some believe that there are times when a Christian just has to go to war. This is because they believe the result of not going to war will be much worse.

Some difficult sayings

 You have heard that it was said, 'An eye for an eye and a tooth for a tooth.' But I say to you, Do not resist one who is evil. But if anyone strikes you on the right cheek, turn to him the other also . . . You have heard that it was said, 'You shall love your neighbour and hate your enemy.' But I say to you, Love your enemies and pray for those who persecute you, so that you may be sons of your Father who is in heaven.

[Matthew 5:38–9, 43–5]

 Blessed are the peacemakers, for they shall be called sons of God.

[Matthew 5:9]

Christian pacifists see these passages as clear-cut evidence that Jesus was opposed to war, whatever the cost might be to ourselves.

Those who take a different view say that Jesus was not referring to conflict between nations but between individuals. Jesus does not talk about what you do when *someone else* is being made to suffer and not you personally.

What is clear, however, is that Jesus preached about peace and when he himself suffered violence and was arrested he prevented his followers from resisting.

War and the Christian Church

 For we no longer take sword against a nation, nor do we learn any more to make war, having become sons of peace for the sake of Jesus who is our leader.

[Origen, *c.* 185–254 CE]

From these words of Origen, who was an early Christian writer, it seems that in its early days the Church was pacifist. But from the fourth century CE onwards, Christianity became the State religion and Christians joined the Roman army.

On page 118 you will have read the description of the 'Just War', as laid down by the famous medieval Christian teacher, Thomas Aquinas. This shows that the Church had developed a kind of 'doctrine of war'.

Nowadays it is impossible to think of war without also considering the issue of nuclear weapons, and many Christian groups who would not have been pacifist before feel that nuclear weapons change everything and they must be totally opposed to war.

▼ **In small groups discuss the problems Christians have about deciding these questions:**
Is war ever the lesser of two evils?
Read how Jesus cleared the money changers from the Temple in John 2:13–15. Does this incident show that Jesus felt violence was justified under certain circumstances?
Is it possible to 'turn the other cheek' when someone you love is in great danger?

ॐ Hinduism

Hinduism is concerned with the inner spiritual life of the soul (atman) and with the fulfilment of sacred law (dharma) in the world.

Bhagavad Gita

The Bhagavad Gita means 'the Song of the Lord'. It is the best-known book in India. It is part of a much longer work called the Mahabharata.

In the Bhagavad Gita, Arjuna the warrior is dismayed when he sees his relations among the enemy ranks. He confesses to Krishna, who is acting as his charioteer, that he cannot fight as he cannot kill his own flesh and blood. During the course of the conversation, which takes up the whole book, Krishna reveals himself to be an incarnation of the god Vishnu. He teaches him that it is his duty, or dharma, as a warrior of the Kshatriya caste to fight. Krishna teaches Arjuna that the soul, or atman, is indestructible. It is eternal, and therefore it does not matter if the body dies. The soul will simply be reborn into another body:

 As a person puts on new garments, giving up old ones, the soul similarly accepts new material bodies, giving up the old and useless ones.   [2:22]

Dharma

The important thing therefore for Hindus is to fulfil one's dharma, or duty. If a Hindu is born into a warrior caste, then his duty is to fight and kill. By perfecting their dharma, Hindus believe that they will be reborn into a higher state in life in the next rebirth. The importance of this doctrine is revealed in the following passage:

 No one should leave the path of dharma on any account – neither by temptation nor by fear nor by greed nor for life. Because pleasure and pain are both transitory [passing], dharma is permanent and follows the soul in all directions.
                    [Mahabharata: Asvamedha Parva 43:14]

In fact, Krishna informs Arjuna that because his enemy are on the side of the wicked, they are as good as dead already:

 I have already slain these men, you are only an instrument.
                    [Bhagavad Gita 11:33]

 One who has taken his birth is sure to die and, after death, one is sure to take birth again. Therefore, in the unavoidable discharge of your duty, you should not lament.   [Bhagavad Gita 2:27]

Arjuna takes great courage in Krishna's words, launches into battle and is victorious.

At a later point in the Bhagavad Gita, Krishna preaches personal devotion to himself as the Supreme Lord, and that this devotion means having no hatred for any being at all:

 Do works for Me, make Me thy highest goal, Be loyal in love to Me,
Cast off all other attachments, Have no hatred for any being at all:
For all who do thus shall come to Me.   [11:55]

Spiritual battles

Many of the gods and heroes in the Hindu scriptures fight in epic battles. The most famous of these is Prince Rama who, like Krishna, is an incarnation of Vishnu. He comes to earth to fight the dreadful demon king Ravana. (You may wish to read about the heroic deeds of Rama in the Ramayana.) Often these battles have a spiritual nature. They are myths, which show an inward fight, and teach values that are true for all time.

▼ **Can you think of any modern stories which, like the Ramayana, show the triumph of good over evil? In your examples, is violence used, and is it justified? Give your reasons.**

▼ **Draw a diagram to illustrate the Hindu belief of reincarnation. You may wish to use the images contained in the passage: 'As a person puts on new garments . . . '.**

Arjuna in his chariot before the battle. Who is the figure in his chariot disguised as a charioteer?

RELIGIONS

Gandhi

One of the most famous Hindu personalities was Mohandas Gandhi. He was nicknamed 'Mahatma', which means the 'Great Soul', and was one of the most influential figures of the twentieth century. He is known primarily for his commitment to non-violent action against British rule in India which helped India to gain its independence in 1947.

Jainism began in India at about the same time as the birth of Buddhism. Jains still exist today. They are noted for their strict vegetarianism and care in daily life to avoid harming any living creature. This photograph shows Jains with a cloth covering their mouths to prevent the swallowing of tiny life-forms. What is the man carrying in his right hand? What do you think it is for?

Gandhi was deeply influenced as a child by the teachings of the Jain religion on *ahimsa* (non-violence). He also saw this in Jesus' Sermon on the Mount (Matthew 5–7 – see page 154). In his life he began to experiment to see if these spiritual ideas could be lived out, especially within the world of politics.

Satyagraha – the force of truth

Gandhi's starting point was the belief that God and Truth were one and the same. There was nothing new in this idea: it was part of Hindu thinking. What was new was Gandhi's belief that the 'force of truth' (satyagraha) could be used to fight social injustice. He used it in South Africa to gain better conditions for Asians, and then again in India. His methods were simple. He instructed those around him to meet violence with non-violence and non-co-operation. He and his followers marched, fasted, went to prison, prayed, and went on strike until they convinced the British Government and world opinion that India belonged to the people of India.

When the Indians began fighting among themselves, Gandhi immediately withdrew from all activity and fasted until they stopped. He was prepared to fast until death if necessary in order to teach his people that violence only brought more violence.

Gandhi's non-violent campaign succeeded in removing British rule from India, but he was heartbroken to see the creation of two separate States: Hindu India and Muslim Pakistan. His love for all people ultimately cost him his life. He was assassinated by a fellow Hindu because his love extended to Muslims as well as Hindus. Gandhi saw humanity as one, the world as one family.

Here are some of Gandhi's sayings on ahimsa (non-violence):

> Non-violence is more powerful than all the armaments in the world. It is mightier than the mightiest weapon of destruction devised by the ingenuity of man.

> Non-violence is not passivity in any shape or form. It is the most active force in the world.

> The first principle of non-violent action is that of non-co-operation with everything humiliating.

> In non-violence the masses have a weapon which enables a child, a woman, or even a decrepit old man to resist the mightiest government successfully.

▼ **Take some of these sayings and discuss them in small groups. The following questions might help:**
How can non-violence be 'more powerful than all the armaments in the world'?
How can non-violence be 'the most active force in the world'?
Will non-violence always be successful?

▼ **Martin Luther King was an outstanding Christian leader for the rights of black people in the USA. He was very much influenced by the techniques of non-violence used by Gandhi. Find out more about Martin Luther King's life and compare his campaign with Gandhi's.**

 # Islam

Let there be no compulsion in religion

> 66 Islam is an Arabic word. It is derived from two roots, one *salm*, meaning peace, and the other *SLM*, meaning submission. Islam stands for a 'commitment to surrender one's will to the will of God' and as such be at peace with the Creator and all that has been created by Him. It is through submission to the will of God that peace is produced. [Islamic Council of Europe]

The following passages from the Qur'an do not permit the use of violence to convert people to Islam:

> 66 Invite all to the way of your Lord with wisdom and beautiful preaching and argue with them in ways that are best and most gracious. For your Lord knows best who have strayed from His Path and who receive Guidance. [16:125]

> 66 Let there be no compulsion in religion. Truth stands out clear from error. [2:256]

> 66 If it had been your Lord's Will, they would all have believed – all who are on earth. Will you then compel mankind against their will to believe? [10:99]

Jihad

'Jihad' is the Arabic word used by Muslims to describe the struggle against evil. It also describes the effort to promote and establish the Muslim way of life. The striving is not for oneself but 'in the way of Allah'. Jihad does not mean 'war', but performing 'jihad' can lead a Muslim to fight if it is in the cause of Allah. It may mean giving one's life for Islam.

> 66 And those who are slain in the way of God, He will not send their works astray . . . He will admit them to Paradise, that He has made known to them. [Qur'an 47:7]

Every individual, Muslim or non-Muslim, has the right to practise the religion of their choice. If someone tries to suppress a people's religious freedom, then war, though terrible, is permitted.

> 66 To those against whom war is made, permission is given to fight, because they are wronged, and truly Allah is most powerful for their aid. They are those who have been expelled from their homes in defiance of right – for no reason except that they say: 'Our Lord is Allah.' [Qur'an 22:39–40]

Rules of war

> 66 Fight in the way of God with those who fight with you, but aggress not: God loves not the aggressors. [Qur'an 2:187]

This means that Muslims must not be the first to attack.

In addition, the Hadith forbid Muslim soldiers to kill women, children, the elderly, the disabled and the inhabitants of monasteries. Also the dead bodies of enemy soldiers were not to be mutilated.

Mercy and peace

Once the fighting is over, then mercy is to be shown.

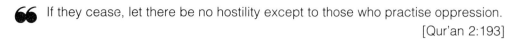 If they cease, let there be no hostility except to those who practise oppression. [Qur'an 2:193]

Further, if war has to be fought, the aim should nevertheless be to return to peace.

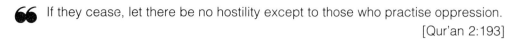 If the enemy inclines towards peace, then you should also incline towards peace and trust in Allah, for He is that hears and knows all. [Qur'an 8:61]

▼ **Compare the Muslim rules about war with the 'Just War' principles on page 118. Set it out clearly.**

▼ **The Crusades were fought first of all because the Muslims were occupying the holy places in Palestine. Christians and Muslims fought each other bitterly. Why did both sides think they were right? You will need to find out something more about the Crusades before writing your answer.**

One way in which Muslims show their commitment to the will of God is in the regular performance of prayer, five times a day

R E L I G I O N S

✡ Judaism

War

In the early days of the ancient nation of Israel, war was seen as a religious duty. The laws laid down who could be excused military service. They included men who had just built a new house or had just got married. There were also rituals by which soldiers were sanctified before the battle.

The idea of war as a religious duty continues in modern Judaism, although it is seen as a last resort.

The rabbis said there were three kinds of war allowed:

1 Wars which were obligatory.
2 Wars which were commanded by God.
3 Wars which were 'discretionary'.

The first category applies only to a war of clear defence against an attack already launched.

Most rabbis agreed that wars in the second category were very few in number. In fact they said there were only two of them: when Joshua fought a war of conquest against the seven nations of Canaan, and the campaign against Amalek (directly commanded by God) (see 1 Samuel 15:3).

A Jewish soldier in prayer at the Western Wall in Jerusalem. The wall is what remains of the ancient temple and has become a specially sacred place for Jews

There is no complete agreement about 'discretionary' wars. Generally it refers to 'preventive' wars, that is, when the State tries to be a 'jump ahead' of an attack which is coming. The following extract is typical of the interpretation of many rabbis:

<blockquote>
 No war may be waged against a nation that has not attacked Israel, or that lives up to the fundamentals of the Universal Religion.
</blockquote>

This author goes on to say that this really means that the permission to fight a *milhemet reshut* (Hebrew for a 'discretionary war'), could only apply when the boundaries of Israel were threatened.

There are also in the Jewish tradition many rules to prevent unnecessary injuries and deaths. Here is a typical one:

<blockquote>
 When siege is laid to a city for the purpose of capture, it may not be surrounded on all four sides but only on three in order to give an opportunity for escape to those who would flee to save their lives. [Maimonides Code]
</blockquote>

The hope of peace

Jews look forward to a time of peace and harmony between all people. *Shalom* is the Hebrew word for peace and is used as a Jewish greeting.

<blockquote>
It shall come to pass in the latter days . . .
He shall judge between the nations,
and shall decide for many peoples;
and they shall beat their swords into ploughshares,
and their spears into pruning hooks;
nation shall not lift up sword against nation,
neither shall they learn war any more. [Isaiah 2:2,4]
</blockquote>

This hope for peace is reflected in a beautifully poetic passage in Isaiah in which the conflicts in the natural world also are at an end. Look it up in Isaiah 11:6–7.

Peace and justice

In Jewish thinking, peace is strongly linked with the idea of justice. That is to say, the reason for the absence of peace is because of the absence of justice.

<blockquote>
 The sword comes to the world because of delay of justice and through perversion of justice. [Talmud]
</blockquote>

▼ **One definition of 'justice' might be 'absolute fairness'. Do you think fairness is important? Can you think of times when there has been quarrelling about justice in this sense? Do you think it is ever possible to be *absolutely* fair? Write a few words about this last question.**

▼ **Do you think there will ever be a period of peace as Isaiah foretold? If so, what do you think it will be like?**

Sikhism

The Khalsa

> Thus the Guru reasoned … His followers were to emerge as splendid warriors, their uncut hair bound in turbans; and as warriors all were to bear the name 'Singh' [lion].
>
> He devised a form of baptism administered with the sword, one which would create a Khalsa staunch and unyielding. His followers would destroy the empire, each Sikh horseman believing himself to be a king.
>
> All weakness would be beaten out of them and each, having taken the baptism of the sword, would thereafter be firmly attached to the sword.

Guru Gobind Singh, the last of the ten Gurus, who said that after him the sacred book should be the Guru of the Sikhs

The passage opposite refers to the time when the tenth Guru (Guru Gobind Singh) organised the Sikhs into an effective army in order to defend their religion from the Muslim Mogul Empire. The previous Guru (Guru Tegh Bahadur) had been executed by Aurangzeb, the Muslim leader, and Guru Gobind Singh saw that in order for Sikhism to survive they needed strength and unity. He therefore chose five brave followers in a dramatic ceremony to form the brotherhood of Sikhs known as the Khalsa. He succeeded in forming a highly skilled and courageous army which halted the expansion of Aurangzeb's empire. Many of the military elements survive to this day, though the struggle is now more of a spiritual nature.

▼ **Look at the picture. What does it tell you about the Guru? Can you also tell what his followers felt about him?**

Defence

Sikhs should never be the first to draw the sword. War should only take place as a last resort – in order to defend the weak and to promote the cause of liberty. (See also page 164.) Guru Gobind Singh shows his acceptance of the 'Just War' principles in one of his writings:

 When all efforts to restore peace prove useless and no words avail,
Lawful is the flash of steel, it is right to draw the sword.

Peace

In one of Guru Gobind Singh's prayers, peace is seen to come from God. It is a gift from God's mercy and therefore to be desired above violence:

 O Kind Father, loving Father, through thy mercy we have spent our day in peace and happiness; grant that we may, according to thy will, do what is right.

The following prayer, which is also a prayer for peace, comes from the Adi Granth which was largely composed by Guru Arjan (the fifth of the ten Gurus). It reveals that real peace is only to be found in God who is the 'haven of peace':

 Great is thy glory, for great is thy name.
Great is thy glory, for thy justice is true.
Great is thy glory, for eternal is the seat.
Great is thy glory, for thou divinest our inner thoughts.
Great is thy glory, for thou givest unasked,
Great is thy glory, for thou art all-in-all.
The Lord is the giver;
The Lord is the haven of peace;
The peace that reigns on snow-clad mountains.   [Adi Granth]

▼ **Find out more about the formation of the Khalsa by Guru Gobind Singh and about the five k's.**

▼ **Do you agree that violence should only be a last resort? Can you think of any military disadvantage in such a view?**

RELIGIONS

▼ General assignments

All religions stress the importance of peace, whether it is for the individual believer or for the creation of a peaceful society. At the same time we live in a violent world and religious groups respond differently in the way they tackle this difficult issue.

▼ **If it is possible, ask your teacher to invite some representatives of religions to discuss with your class what they feel about war and violence and how their religion would help them to know how to act.**

▼ **If a group of people belonging to one religion were under threat of violence, how should they react? Choose one or more of the religions mentioned in this book and compose a statement giving advice as if you were the leader(s). Remember you need to give *religious* reasons for your advice. Choose religions which are not familiar. You may need to read further (see the Further Reading section at the end of this book), and you may find it helpful to consult followers of a particular religion.**

Neve Shalom/Wahat al-Salam (NS/WAS) is an Israeli village between Jerusalem and Tel Aviv. The name of this community means 'oasis of peace' in Hebrew and Arabic. It is a community in which Jews, Muslims and Christians have chosen to live together. One has only to take note of the many newspaper reports on the Arab-Israeli conflict to appreciate that NS/WAS is unique. At the time of writing there are about 75 residents, consisting of 16 families, over 30 children and single members, from the three different religions. When Father Bruno Hussar was asked why people came to live in fairly primitive conditions at NS/WAS he replied:

66 They could not tolerate living in a country where two peoples, each with their own identity, made war on each other, neither of them recognising the other's rights. They want to do something to make reconciliation possible, to break down the barriers of fear, prejudice, ignorance and selfishness which separate the different communities: to build bridges of dialogue.

The most important work of NS/WAS is with children. More than one hundred schools visit the Peace School to spend two or three days in the extraordinary atmosphere created there. Father Bruno commenting on these visits said.

66 By living together, the basis for new human relationships is formed little by little. But at the end of a visit it is often difficult to recognise who is a Jew and who is an Arab, and often tears are shed on parting. However, although it is hard to see the difference, the differences remain; what is important is that they have learned to accept them and to understand them. Sometimes on returning home they are able to convince their parents too, and it is not unusual then for a Jewish family to invite an Arab family (or vice versa) to spend their holidays together.

Israeli Palestinians and Jews take part in a workshop organised by NS/WAS. They are trying to communicate by non-verbal means (in this case drawing) in order to overcome the language barrier. If different peoples had more opportunity to meet each other when young, do you think it would reduce the amount of conflict in the world?

The spirit of NS/WAS is beginning to spill out to other areas of conflict. Catholic and Protestant youth workers from Northern Ireland attended a workshop at NS/WAS, following on workshops given by counsellors of the NS/WAS School for Peace in Derry in Northern Ireland. With regards to this initiative Father Bruno summed up:

66 Our hope is to form a new generation which has learned to be open to others. Perhaps a new generation will be able to achieve that peace which its parents, at present, cannot achieve because their wounds are too deep.

▼ **Discuss these questions in small groups:**
Do you think it is important for people of different religions to meet together?
Can you think of any special reasons why different religions should want to meet together since the end of the Second World War?
Do you think there is any value in praying together for peace?
Why do you think NS/WAS devotes most of its energies to working with young people rather than adults?

▼ **Try to find information about other peace projects such as Corrymeela. (See the list of addresses.) Prepare a short presentation on several or a longer study on one of them.**

▼ 5 Capital Punishment

▼ Introduction

Capital punishment means putting a person to death as a punishment for a crime, for example murder.

The way of doing this varies. In Britain it was by hanging by a rope – until the death penalty was abolished for all murders in 1965 (but see page 146). In many States of the USA the method is by electrocution in specially designed 'electric chairs'. In other States it is carried out by lethal injections of drugs. In some other nations firing squads are used.

A public hanging in Smithfield, London in 1761. Why did people come to see a public hanging? What would your reaction be?

These things are horrible and distressing, and feelings about execution can be very strong. Look at the picture and think for a little just how much strong feelings can influence the way you judge things. Do you think such feelings should influence your judgement about the rights and wrongs of this matter?

▼   **Form groups of three or four and talk to each other about the feelings you have about the death penalty. This discussion is meant to start you thinking, so do not try to come to conclusions or solve all the problems. Just help each other to sort out what is important to you.**

▼   **Choose one person in each group to write down the opinions of the group in two columns – one headed 'Reasons *for* the death penalty', and the other headed 'Reasons *against* the death penalty'. Keep your list so that you can refer to it when your study of this chapter is finished.**

Why should we punish people?

To sort out our thoughts on capital punishment, we need to think first of all about *punishment* itself.

▼   **This time, working in pairs, write down all the reasons you can think of why people should be punished for doing wrong or for breaking the law. You might think, for example, that people should not get away with stealing others' property, or that society has got to protect itself. Place the book on one side until you have finished this. If there is an opportunity, the class might share views on this topic before going further.**

How many of the following reasons did you write down?

1 People who do wrong just ought to be punished. They should get what they deserve. (The word for this is *retribution*.)
2 Punishment keeps people from doing the same crime again and keeps other people from breaking the law. (The word for this is *deterrence*.)
3 Locking people up keeps them from harming more people. (The word for this is *protection*.)
4 Punishment shouldn't be just to make people suffer for what they have done. It should try to make them better and more useful members of society. If nothing happens to them, how will they get any better? (The word for this is *reformation*.)

The four main reasons for punishment

You may have used other words, but the four words used in the brackets are useful to learn if you do not know them already.

1 *Retribution* (people getting what they deserve)
2 *Deterrence* (stopping people from doing the same crime again)
3 *Protection* (stopping people from harming others)
4 *Reformation* (helping those who have done wrong to become better people)

▼   **In groups, and then as a class, see if you can agree upon an order of importance for these four reasons for punishment.**

▼ **Retribution**

Here are four ways in which the case for the death penalty is sometimes put:

> 66 It is essential that murderers get their 'come-uppance'. People would just do what they like if we didn't punish killers with death.

> 66 We simply cannot allow that sort of thing to happen. If certain kinds of murderers get away with it, then we shall lose all sense of right and wrong.

> 66 Human beings live together. The ability to live together in a community depends on everybody having the same ideas of right and wrong. This is even more important in the case of murder, because it threatens to destroy the community. To keep clear what it thinks the worst crime is, the community has to speak very loudly. The death penalty is the only way that a community can 'speak' loudly enough.

> 66 We should have an eye for an eye and a tooth for a tooth.

These are arguments for capital punishment as *retribution.*

Those who are *against* the retribution view of capital punishment fall into two groups:

1 Those who are against it 'at all costs', because it is wrong to kill a human being in any circumstances. So it is not right to kill for punishment either – not even a murderer.
2 Those who oppose the idea of execution, not because the murderer does not 'deserve' to die, but because an execution is so much worse than murder.

Here is a quotation from Benazir Bhutto whose father was executed in Pakistan:

> 66 They hanged my father in the early hours of 4 April 1979 inside Rawalpindi Central Jail. Imprisoned with my mother a few miles away in a deserted police training camp at Sihala, I felt the moment of my father's death. Despite the valium my mother had given me to try to get through the agonising night, I suddenly sat bolt-upright in bed at 2 a.m. 'No!' I couldn't breathe, didn't want to breathe. Papa! Papa! I felt cold, so cold, in spite of the heat, and couldn't stop shaking.

▼ **Do you think the people in the second group have a point? In what ways might execution be worse then murder? Write down what you think and your reasons.**

Many people also feel that because mistakes have been made in the courts, the risk of executing anyone for a murder they did not commit is not acceptable.

▼ **There have been cases of innocent people being executed for crimes they did not commit. As a piece of individual research, find out as much as you can about one person and write about it. You might also make a wall display.**

(right) Death row in Huntsville, Texas in 1981. There were 158 inmates waiting to die; most were also waiting for the results of court appeals. How do you react to this picture?

▼ Deterrence, protection or reformation?

New vote likely on hanging next year

Most people think that capital punishment deters people from committing murder.

▼ **You could test this by carrying out a survey of your year or another group. Make and duplicate questionnaires like the one below, or go out and ask people personally using the same questions.**

Questionnaire

Put a tick against the appropriate answer.

1   Do you think murderers should be executed?   Yes ☐   No ☐

2   Do you think fear of execution stops people from committing murder?

                                                         Yes ☐   No ☐

When you have collected all the answers you can compare the answers to the two questions and test the statement at the top of this page.

▼ **With the help of your teacher you could try more complicated surveys, or compare answers from different groups (such as boys and girls); but remember that your sample is likely to be quite small and you must not claim too much for your results!**

Official surveys

Figures are collected in official surveys about whether capital punishment has any effect on the number of murders. They do not give a definite answer. Rates are compared before and after capital punishment has been abolished in a country. Or rates are compared in different countries. These figures do not support the argument that capital punishment stops murders more than other forms of punishment.

Some people feel that, whether you can *prove* that capital punishment 'works' or not, it seems better to give the death penalty the benefit of the doubt. This is sometimes called the 'best bet' argument!

Does the death penalty protect the public?

The figures show that even if a country has a death penalty it does not put a stop to murders. The figures cannot even show that the death penalty makes murder happen less often. Some feel, however, that execution at least makes sure that particular individuals can never again commit the same crime.

There are very few occasions when a murderer has killed again after escaping from prison. Most of those who have done so were insane – and those who have been proved insane would not have been executed in the first place. Not many people would suggest that we ought to execute the mentally ill.

Town haunted by doubts over hanged man

What about terrorism?

Many countries have suffered in this century from what is called 'terrorism'. Those who are called terrorists are those who feel strong opposition to the government in power and feel that they cannot change anything by peaceful means. Often they will carry out killings in order to 'frighten' a government into giving them what they think is just.

This is a little different from other kinds of murders and sometimes governments introduce the death penalty for terrorist crimes. But people who do these killings feel they have a just cause and there is only one course of action open to them. The effect of executing them when they are caught is to turn them into martyrs – people to be admired for devotion to their cause. This attracts new recruits to their ranks, who are willing to risk their own lives.

Does punishment reform wrongdoers?

The 'reformation' argument is that punishment is necessary as a way of making the offender 'better'. There is not much evidence that the punishments given to people are very successful in changing them for the better. However, in some places an effort is being made to find the kinds of treatment which will be of benefit to these individuals as well as to society.

But this can have no meaning in the case of capital punishment – unless one believes that paying the penalty in this life improves matters in an afterlife. This might apply in some religions. (It was the view taken by some Christian courts in the Middle Ages, called the 'Inquisition'.) It is felt that by making sure the offender suffers the proper human punishment, so God will have mercy on the person's soul.

▼ **Find out about at least one other form of punishment for criminals besides imprisonment, and write a report.**

▼ Checklist of countries

The following lists show the state of the law in almost all countries as regards the death penalty in 1989.

Countries where the death penalty is abolished for all crimes

	Date		Date		Date
Australia	1985	Germany		Nicaragua	1979
Austria	1968	(Federal Republic)	1949	Norway	1979
Cape Verde	1981	Haiti	1987	Panama	
Colombia	1910	Honduras	1956	Philippines	1987
Costa Rica	1877	Iceland	1928	Portugal	1976
Denmark	1978	Kiribati		San Marino	1865
Dominican Republic	1966	Liechtenstein	1987	Solomon Islands	
Ecuador	1906	Luxembourg	1979	Sweden	1972
Finland	1972	Marshall Islands		Tuvalu	
France	1981	Micronesia		Uruguay	1907
German Democratic		(Federated States)		Vanuatu	
Republic	1987	Monaco	1962	Vatican City State	1969
		Netherlands	1982	Venezuela	1863

Total: 35 countries

Countries where the death penalty is abolished *except* for certain crimes under military law or crimes committed in exceptional circumstances such as wartime

	Date		Date		Date
Argentina	1984	Israel	1954	Peru	1979
Brazil	1979	Italy	1947	São Tomé and Principe	
Canada	1976	Malta	1971	Seychelles	
Cyprus	1983	Mexico		Spain	1978
El Salvador	1983	New Zealand	1961	Switzerland	1942
Fiji	1979	Papua New Guinea	1974	United Kingdom	1973

Total: 18 countries

▼ **That makes 53 countries where there is basically no capital punishment. Is this more or less than you expected? Does any name in the above two lists come as a surprise to you? If so, why?**

United States of America

Thirty-six States of the USA have the death penalty but some make use of it more than others. In 1990 there were 2,331 people awaiting execution in the USA. Between 1976 and 1990 there were 121 executions. In some States prisoners have been waiting under sentence for many years. This is because of appeals being fought out in the courts.

▼ **Discuss with some others the effect of such long waits on prisoners.**

Countries and territories whose laws provide for the death penalty for ordinary crimes

Some of the countries below have not carried out executions in recent years. A 1980 United Nations study listed four countries which had not carried out executions for the past 40 years. In some countries the position seems to rest on a personal decision by the Governor or President not to allow executions to be carried out. They do this in spite of the fact that public opinion would support the death penalty being kept.

Afghanistan
Albania
Algeria
Andorra
Angola
Anguilla
Antigua and
 Barbuda
Bahamas
Bahrain
Bangladesh
Barbados
Belgium
Belize
Benin
Bermuda
Bhutan
Bolivia
Botswana
British Virgin
 Islands
Brunei
 Darussalam
Bulgaria
Burkina Faso
Burma
Burundi
Cameroon
Cayman Islands
Central African
 Republic
Chad
Chile
China (People's
 Republic)
Comoros
Congo
Côte d'Ivoire

Cuba
Czechoslovakia
Djibouti
Dominica
Egypt
Equatorial Guinea
Ethiopia
Gabon
Gambia
Ghana
Greece
Grenada
Guatemala
Guinea
Guinea-Bissau
Guyana
Hong Kong
Hungary
India
Indonesia
Iran
Iraq
Ireland
Jamaica
Japan
Jordan
Kampuchea
Kenya
Korea
 (Democratic
 People's
 Republic)
Korea (Republic)
Kuwait
Laos
Lebanon
Lesotho
Liberia

Libya
Madagascar
Malawi
Malaysia
Maldives
Mali
Mauritania
Mauritius
Mongolia
Montserrat
Morocco
Mozambique
Namibia
Nauru
Nepal
Niger
Nigeria
Oman
Pakistan
Paraguay
Poland
Qatar
Romania
Rwanda
Saint
 Christopher
 and Nevis
Saint Lucia
Saint Vincent
 and the
 Grenadines
Saudi Arabia
Senegal
Sierra Leone
Singapore
Somalia
South Africa
Sri Lanka

Sudan
Suriname
Swaziland
Syria
Taiwan (Republic
 of China)
Tanzania
Thailand
Togo
Tonga
Trinidad
 and Tobago
Tunisia
Turkey
Turks
 and Caicos
 Islands
Uganda
Union of Soviet
 Socialist
 Republics
United
 Arab Emirates
United States of
 America
Viet Nam
Western Samoa
Yemen (Arab
 Republic)
Yemen(People's
 Democratic
 Republic)
Yugoslavia
Zaire
Zambia
Zimbabwe

Total: 127 countries and territories

Twenty-two countries allow the death penalty for drug offences and in some it is mandatory (that is, the person *must* be executed if found guilty). Among the latter are: Malaysia (at least 62 such executions between 1975 and 1988), Taiwan, Iran (over 300 such executions between January and April 1989), Singapore and China.

▼ **Discuss with others anything of interest in this last list. For example, why do you think some countries feel that the death penalty is necessary for drug offences, and do you think they are justified?**

▼ Opposing views

Here are two quotations which might help in your consideration of the issue of capital punishment.

Death is a greater deterrent

Sir Ian Percival MP believes there should be capital punishment for those convicted of premeditated murder. In presenting the Criminal Justice Bill to the House of Commons in 1987 he said:

 Perhaps I could remind the House of one aspect of the sentence of life imprisonment. If it means what it says – and unless it does it is not much of a deterrent – it is a fierce punishment. It means locking up a person for the rest of his natural life, killing him at whatever speed it takes him to die. One might even ask if it is any more humane.

Of course, those who oppose the death penalty suggest that if we ask convicted criminals which they would rather have they will invariably choose life imprisonment. So they would, almost invariably, but surely that only serves to confirm the view of those who agree with me that the vast majority fear death more than they fear life imprisonment. That is why they would rather have life imprisonment than death. So it is a greater deterrent to those who can be deterred, not a complete deterrent but demonstrably a greater deterrent than life imprisonment. That leads in my view to but one conclusion.

▼ **Write Sir Ian Percival's argument in your own words. What is the 'one conclusion' referred to in the last sentence?**

Prisoner to the gallows

Here is a quotation from George Orwell's *Collected Essays* in which he recalls the experience he once had escorting a prisoner to the gallows in Burma in 1931:

 We set out for the gallows. Two warders marched on either side of the prisoner, with their rifles at the slope; two others marched close against him, gripping him by arm and shoulder, as though at once pushing and supporting him. The rest of us, magistrates and the like, followed behind.

Suddenly, when we had gone ten yards, the procession stopped short without any order or warning. A dreadful thing had happened – a dog, come goodness knows whence, had appeared in the yard. It came bounding among us with a loud volley of barks and leapt round us wagging its whole body, wild with glee at finding so many human beings together. It was a large woolly dog, half Airedale, half pariah. For a moment it pranced round us, and then before anyone could stop it, it made a dash for the prisoner, and jumping up tried to lick his face. Everybody stood aghast, too taken aback even to grab the dog.

'Who let that bloody brute in here?' said the superintendent angrily. 'Catch it someone!' . . .

A warder detached from the escort, charged clumsily after the dog, but it danced and gambolled just out of his reach, taking everything as part of the game. A young Eurasian jailer picked up a handful of gravel and tried to stone the dog away, but it dodged the stones and came after us again. Its yaps echoed from the jail walls. The prisoner, in the grasp of the two warders, looked on incuriously, as though this was another formality of the hanging. It was several minutes before someone managed to catch the dog. Then we put my handkerchief through its collar and moved off once more, with the dog still straining and whimpering.

It was about forty yards to the gallows. I watched the bare brown back of the prisoner marching in front of me. He walked clumsily with his bound arms, but quite steadily, with that bobbing gait of the Indian who never straightens his knees. At each step his muscles slid neatly into place, the lock of hair on his scalp danced up and down, his feet printed themselves on the wet gravel. And once in spite of the men who gripped him by each shoulder, he stepped slightly aside to avoid a puddle in the path.

It is curious, but till that moment I had never realised what it means to destroy a healthy, conscious man. When I saw the prisoner step aside to avoid the puddle I saw the mystery, the unspeakable wrongness, of cutting a life short when it is in full tide. This man was not dying, was alive just as we are alive. All the organs of his body were working – bowels digesting food, skin renewing itself, nails growing, tissues forming – all toiling away in solemn foolery. His nails would still be growing when he stood on the drop, when he was falling through the air with a tenth-of-a-second to live. His eyes saw the yellow gravel and the grey walls, and his brain still remembered, foresaw, reasoned – even about puddles. He and we were a party of men walking together, seeing, hearing, feeling, understanding the same world; and in two minutes, with a sudden snap, one of us would be gone – one mind less, one world less.

▼ **Why do you think George Orwell describes the dog coming in as 'a dreadful thing'?**

▼ **Think about the sentence, 'When I saw the prisoner step aside to avoid the puddle I saw the mystery . . . '. Try to put in your own words what he meant.**

Capital Punishment: Religions

RELIGIONS

▼ Rules and views

There are two main ways in which religion influences the way some people think when they are trying to decide whether capital punishment is right or wrong. (See also page 165.)

1 Religions have rules or commandments which are believed to have absolute or divine authority. For example, 'You shall not kill'. In some religions death is prescribed for certain crimes.
2 Religions also have teachings or doctrines about what human beings are supposed to be like. They may say, for example, that human beings are in a special relationship with God.

In the Sikh scriptures it says:

 God lives in everything,
He dwells in every heart.   [Guru Arjan]

Because of this, actions which hurt or kill human beings might be thought to be wrong. Decisions are affected by the view taken of the meaning and purpose of life.

So it is not just a matter of looking for rules written in scriptures that matters. We also have to try to understand what the important doctrines are. This is especially true of the question of putting people to death, because it is such an extreme thing to do. Putting someone to death judicially, must mean at least having a philosophy about the position of an individual in society.

Followers of all the religions studied here are divided in their views. One difficulty is that the same statement can lead to different conclusions. For example, the statement that human beings are made by God, which appears in most religions, can lead to quite opposite conclusions about the death penalty. On the one hand some interpret it to mean that because God made human beings we should on no account take a life – even for murder. On the other hand it is argued that human life is so precious that anyone who kills deliberately *must* in turn be put to death! It is therefore important to remember when reading the texts from various sources that much will depend on the particular way it is understood.

> ▼ **Discuss in a small group which side *you* would take in the debate in the previous paragraph. That is, does the belief that God created human beings make the death penalty for murder more justified or less?**

Another aspect which could influence decisions is what each religion believes happens after death. Some religions, for example, consider that our souls are reborn in new bodies. Others believe that there is a divine judgement which follows death.

▼ **Turn back to the section on pages 6–7 and, before reading any further, write down briefly what position you think might be adopted in each religion in relation to the death penalty.**

The burning of three Protestant 'heretics' at Norwich in 1558. Do you think this is realistic? What does the artist think about the people being burned?

⊕ Buddhism

The first precept

The five basic precepts of Buddhism are listed on page 66. The most important from the point of view of capital punishment is the first: 'I undertake to observe the rule to abstain from taking life.' (This is extended sometimes to 'abstain from harming others.')

About 400 CE a famous teacher called Buddhaghosa wrote about Buddhist teaching. Here are some passages in which he writes about the first precept, about the act of murder, and about ways of killing.

Taking life

 'Taking life' means to kill anything that lives. The precept says that you should not strike or kill any living being. 'Anything that lives' is anything that has what is called the 'life-force'. This includes all members of the animal kingdom as well as humans. 'Taking life' means killing or trying to kill *deliberately*, by word or action.

With regard to animals, it is worse to kill large ones than small ones. This is because you have to make a much greater effort to kill large ones. Even where the effort is the same, the difference in *importance* has to be taken into account. When it comes to human beings, the killing is considered to be worse if the person killed was a good (virtuous) person. Apart from that, the seriousness of the offence is also measured by how much the murderer *wanted* the killing to happen.

The act of murder

 Five factors are involved:
1 There is a living being.
2 There is the perception of a living being
   (i.e. by someone else).
3 There is the *thought* of murder.
4 There is the *action* of carrying it out.
5 There is death as a result of the action.

Six ways of killing

 There are six ways of carrying out the killing:
1 with one's own hand
2 by using someone else
3 by slow poisoning
4 by using missiles (stones)
5 by sorcery
6 by psychic power

Buddhism is totally against the taking of life under any circumstances, though, in practice, the death penalty does exist in some Buddhist countries, for example Thailand and Burma.

▼ Look again at Buddhaghosa's commentary above, and write down your answers to the following questions:

a) What do you think he means by 'the life-force'?

b) He considers that *wanting* to kill is very important in judging this action. Do you agree? Give your reasons.

c) What do you think of the distinctions Buddhaghosa makes between killing:

large and small animals?

good people and 'less good' people?

d) Buddhaghosa defines wrongful killing in the 'five factors' above. Do you think this is useful? Give your reasons.

e) Buddhaghosa was writing about 400 CE. How would the list of 'six ways' be different if he were writing nowadays?

Buddhist monks keep five more basic rules in addition to the five precepts on page 66. Can you find out what they are?

✝ Christianity

What Christianity has to say about right and wrong is not discovered simply by turning to a text in the Bible. The Bible gives an account of the 'central events' of the faith and does not deal directly with every single question which may arise.

Christian practice is also guided by a long tradition of teaching in the Church. Some of this teaching has been controversial and disputes have led to divisions of the Church into separate groups.

In the case of capital punishment, the Churches have themselves often pronounced the sentence of death. In perhaps more violent times there have been numerous executions for 'heretics', that is, those considered to be holding wrong or dangerous beliefs. Catholics and Protestants have both persecuted each other in this way. In the present time many Christians have come to hold the view that capital punishment is totally against the spirit of Christian teaching. In rethinking their attitude, Christians try to return to the central event of Christianity which is founded on the coming of Jesus Christ, whom Christians believe to be God. He was executed by the Romans by the method of crucifixion. His rising from the dead to eternal life is central to Christian belief.

What the scriptures say

During the period of the development of Christianity, capital punishment was an accepted part of the legal system and it was more or less taken for granted. Capital punishment continues to be supported by some Christians. There is no direct statement in Christian scriptures which forbids its use.

The Sermon on the Mount

Christians, in trying to make up their minds, take account of the teaching of Jesus, such as the Sermon on the Mount (Matthew 5–7). Here are short extracts:

> You have heard that it was said to the men of old, 'You shall not kill; and whoever kills shall be liable to judgement.' But I say to you that every one who is angry with his brother shall be liable to judgement; whoever insults his brother shall be liable to the council, and whoever says, 'You fool!' shall be liable to the hell of fire. . . .
>
> You have heard that it was said, 'An eye for an eye and a tooth for a tooth.' But I say to you, Do not resist one who is evil. But if anyone strikes you on the right cheek, turn to him the other also; and if anyone would sue you and take your coat, let him have your cloak as well; and if anyone forces you to go one mile, go with him two miles. Give to him who begs from you, and do not refuse him who would borrow from you.
>
> You have heard that it was said, 'You shall love your neighbour and hate your enemy.' But I say to you, Love your enemies and pray for those who persecute you, so that you may be sons of your Father who is in heaven; for he makes his sun rise on the evil and on the good, and sends rain on the just and on the unjust.

[Matthew 5:21–2, 38–45]

▼ **Do you think that Jesus' words here can be put into practice? He suggests that we should not only forgive people who do us wrong but actively love them. Do you think this has anything to do with our thinking about capital punishment? Discuss this with one or two others.**

When Christians argue about the death penalty they will think about three things in particular: what Jesus actually said, his teaching that people should love one another, and that he himself suffered the death penalty.

An early twentieth-century painting, 'Crucifixion with darkened sun' by Schiele. Crucifixion was a Roman method of capital punishment. This particular execution is at the centre of all Christian teaching. Why do you think that the writers of the Christian Gospels felt it important to say 'there was darkness over all the land' when Jesus was crucified?

RELIGIONS

▼

Did Jesus give laws?

Many Christians think that Jesus came to do away with the idea of 'laws' in the usual sense. His words were certainly not meant to become part of the legal system of any country. These Christians argue that Jesus' sayings really express a 'spirit' or an 'attitude'. They were not meant to be used as laws. The Sermon on the Mount, they say, expresses an *ideal* situation, which is a hope for the future. So if you take this view, you cannot just take Jesus' words and say 'There is the Christian position'. You have to understand the spirit of them and work out what they mean for particular situations.

WER VNDER EVCH AN SVND IST
DER WERFFE DEN ERSTEN STEIN AVEF SI
1 5 8 32

'Christ and the woman taken in adultery.' Read John 8:1–11. The German words at the top of the picture are Jesus' words from verse 7: 'Let him who is without sin among you be the first to throw a stone at her.' Do you think these words have anything to do with how we should think of punishment? Why do you think the punishment was death by stoning? How do we view adultery today? It is unlikely that they would have brought a man taken in adultery to Jesus. What do you think about this? This sixteenth-century painting has some very precise portraits. Look carefully and discuss them with others

The 'law' of love

Jesus preached what is sometimes called the 'law of love'. It cannot really be called a 'law', because you cannot *order* someone to love. But you can try to behave in a *loving way* towards other people.

Some Christians would say that this means that sometimes you have to be very severe. It is not loving if you help people avoid the consequences of their actions. Some have argued that by insisting on the death penalty we may be helping someone to the possibility of a better life after death. They will have suffered the proper punishment and cleared the way to being reunited with God. As has already been said, the judges of the medieval church, sometimes called 'Inquisitors', certainly took this view. It would, of course, be wrong to suggest that supporters of the death penalty today take such a stance. Rather, they argue for the death penalty (for murder only) as a matter of 'natural justice'.

Jesus = humanity

Attitudes are also affected by more doctrinal considerations (see page 150). In the case of Christianity, it is not only a matter of looking for authoritative statements or something which can be seen as a command from God. Christians believe that the coming of Jesus Christ changed the whole understanding of human beings and their relationship with God. His identification with humankind means that in our moral judgements we have to go beyond natural instincts, even beyond 'natural justice'.

Many Christians who are against the death penalty might say:

 The execution of Jesus was the greatest evil ever committed by human beings. He was the Son of God and he represents all humanity. Deliberate killing of a prisoner is like crucifying Jesus again.

In the parable known as the Parable of the Last Judgement (Matthew 25:31–46), Jesus teaches his disciples that in the future the way to serve him is to serve the needy:

 'I was hungry and you gave me food, I was thirsty and you gave me drink, I was a stranger and you welcomed me, I was naked and you clothed me, I was sick and you visited me, I was in prison and you came to me.' Then the righteous will answer him, 'Lord, when did we see thee hungry and feed thee, or thirsty and give thee drink? And when did we see thee a stranger and welcome thee, or naked and clothe thee? And when did we see thee sick or in prison and visit thee?' And the King will anwer them, 'Truly, I say to you, as you did it to one of the least of these my brethren, you did it to me.'   [Matthew 25:35–40]

This shows how Jesus is seen as a 'representative' of humanity.

▼   **Discuss in a group or in pairs whether Christians ought to favour the death penalty or not. Try to support your arguments from Christian sources. If it is helpful, you could ask your teacher to invite a local Christian minister to come and give their view.**

▼   **Afterwards write down briefly and fairly the Christian arguments for and against the death penalty for murder.**

Hinduism

Hindus believe that all humans have an immortal soul. 'Immortal' means that it does not die when the body dies. That soul, called *atman*, is then free to enter another body which is being born. Another belief is *karma*. This means that every action has a result. What happens to us is the consequence of our own actions. These actions can be ones which we have done in this present life or in a previous life. For many Hindus the immortal soul, atman, mentioned above, is part of *Brahman*, which is the word for 'ultimate reality' in Hinduism.

Below is a brief quotation from a Hindu scripture called the Vaishnava-dharma-shastra.

The indestructible self

 Kala [time] is no one's friend and no one's enemy: when the effect of his acts in a former existence, by which his present existence is caused, has expired he snatches a man away forcibly. . . .

As a man puts on new clothes in this world, throwing aside those which he formerly wore, even so the self [atman or soul] of man puts on new bodies, which are in accordance with his acts [in a former life].

No weapons will hurt the self of man, no fire burn it, no waters moisten it, and no wind dry it up.

It is not to be hurt, not to be burnt, not to be moistened, and not to be dried up; it is imperishable, perpetual, unchanging, immovable, without beginning.

It is further said to be immaterial, passing all thought, and immutable. Knowing the self [atman] of man to be such, you must not grieve [for the destruction of his body]. [20:43,50–3]

▼ **Read this passage again carefully and write down what it says about the 'self' or 'atman'. What effect might this have on a view of capital punishment?**

Non-violence

Many Hindus believe in non-violence. This view was greatly strengthened by the teaching and example of Mahatma Gandhi (see pages 130–1). The way in which Hindus decide about right and wrong comes from something called *dharma*. This is sometimes translated as 'law'. But it is a little more complicated than that. Each person is born in a particular caste and is therefore expected to live by the laws of that caste. So if you are born in a soldier caste you will be required to kill under certain circumstances. In the famous book, the Bhagavad Gita, this was the dilemma facing Arjuna as he prepared for battle. His instincts told him not to kill but his dharma required him to do it (see pages 128–9).

Here is something Gandhi wrote about non-violence:

 When a person claims to be non-violent, he is expected not to be angry with one who has injured him. He will not wish him harm; he will wish him well; he will not swear at him; he will not cause him any physical hurt. He will put up with all the injury to which he is subjected by the wrong-doer. . . . Non-violence is therefore in its active form goodwill towards all life. It is pure Love. I read it in the Hindu scriptures, in the Bible, in the Qur'an.

RELIGIONS

Mahatma Gandhi in 1939. He is eating his last meal before beginning a fast against British rule in India

▼   **Discuss in pairs whether these words of Gandhi (opposite) have anything to do with the death penalty. Make some notes of your findings.**

Islam

Punishment is only inflicted in Islam when there has been a violation of *other people's* rights. So there is no punishment by humans for not saying your prayers, or not fasting, or not going on prilgrimage, and so on. These are sins committed against God, and in Islam it is considered that God will decide whom he will punish and who is forgiven. Muslims must not declare their sins publicly.

Crimes punishable by death

The Qur'an says that a murderer should be killed. However, the relatives of the victim can sometimes choose compensation from the killer rather than demand his death. (This is usually to cover cases where the killing was not intentional.) It means that the family of the person killed can agree to accept a sum of money, or some valuable goods, from the person responsible or his family. There have been recent cases where the victim's family has been asked by a Muslim court to choose between execution, compensation or freedom for the murderers.

66 O you who believe! The law of retaliation is prescribed for you in the case of murder; a free man (shall die) for a free man, a slave for a slave, a woman for a woman. He who is forgiven by his brother may be prosecuted according to what is just, and he shall pay a liberal fine. This is a merciful dispensation from your Lord. He that transgresses after shall be sternly punished. [Qur'an 2:178]

▼ **Do you think it is a good idea to give the family of the person killed a choice between compensation and execution? Write down the advantages and disadvantages.**

66 This is the penalty of those who fight against God and His Messenger, and hasten about the earth and do corruption there: they shall be slaughtered, or crucified, or one hand and one foot shall be cut off on alternate sides, or they shall be banished from the land. That is the disgrace for them in this world; and in the world to come awaits them a mighty punishment. [Qur'an 5:33]

It is generally understood that fighting 'against God and His Messenger' refers to bandits and murderers who cause disorder in a settled State.

There are four kinds of punishment. Which one is used will depend on the circumstances of the case. If there has been murder in the course of a robbery, the punishment of those guilty would be execution. Where the bandits have been guilty of cruel and violent crimes but have not actually killed, then one of their hands and feet may be cut off. If their crimes are less serious then they may be imprisoned. The punishments are *possible* punishments and do not always have to be carried out. People accused of crimes must be tried in a properly constituted court. According to the laws of Islam, sentences cannot simply be decided by individuals.

▼ **Surah 5 in the Qur'an states: 'Whoso kills a man who has not killed or made trouble in the land, it is as though he had killed mankind altogether.' Try writing in a few words what you think this means.**

 # Judaism

One of the most important ideas in Judaism is the sense of a 'people' or nation. The sacred books of Judaism contain much about the conduct of a nation, as well as laws about how people are to work together and how they should settle their differences. Jews will study these texts carefully and try to apply them to modern situations.

The basic rules

 If there is found among you, within any of your towns which the Lord your God gives you, a man or woman who does what is evil in the sight of the Lord your God, in transgressing his covenant, and has gone and served other gods and worshipped them, or the sun or the moon or any of the host of heaven, which I have forbidden, and it is told you and you hear of it; then you shall inquire diligently, and if it is true and certain that such an abominable thing has been done in Israel, then you shall bring forth to your gates that man or woman who has done this evil thing, and you shall stone that man or woman to death with stones. On the evidence of two witnesses or of three witnesses he that is to die shall be put to death; a person shall not be put to death on the evidence of one witness. The hand of the witnesses shall be first against him to put him to death, and afterward the hand of all the people. So you shall purge the evil from the midst of you.

[Deuteronomy 17:2–7]

Deciding difficult cases

 If any case arises requiring decision between one kind of homicide and another, one kind of legal right and another, or one kind of assault and another, any case within your towns which is too difficult for you, then you shall arise and go up to the place which the Lord your God will choose, and coming to the Levitical priests, and to the judge who is in office in those days, you shall consult them, and they shall declare to you the decision. [Deuteronomy 17:8–9]

Torah and Talmud

These words are taken from the Torah, which is the basic authoritative text for Jews. Another book which has great authority in Judaism is the Talmud. It contains commentaries made by rabbis over a wide range of matters, interpreting the Torah.

The method of execution mentioned in Deuteronomy is by stoning. Other methods mentioned in the Bible are burning and strangling. The Talmud adds slaying by the sword.

Capital crimes

The Torah prescribes the death penalty for murder.

 Whoever strikes a man so that he dies shall be put to death. [Exodus 21:12]

It also allows it for insulting or beating one's parents, adultery, incest, kidnapping, and working on the Sabbath.

RELIGIONS

RELIGIONS

" Whoever strikes his father or his mother shall be put to death. . . . Whoever curses his father or his mother shall be put to death.   [Exodus 21:15,17]

" If a man commits adultery with the wife of his neighbour, both the adulterer and the adulteress shall be put to death.   [Leviticus 20:10]

" The man who lies with his father's wife has uncovered his father's nakedness; both of them shall be put to death, their blood is upon them. If a man lies with his daughter-in-law, both of them shall be put to death; they have committed incest, their blood is upon them.   [Leviticus 20:11–12]

" Whoever steals a man, whether he sells him or is found in possession of him, shall be put to death.   [Exodus 21:16]

" Six days shall work be done, but on the seventh day you shall have a holy sabbath of solemn rest to the Lord; whoever does any work on it shall be put to death; you shall kindle no fire in all your habitations on the sabbath day.   [Exodus 35:2–3]

The rabbis' views

At the time of the writing of the Talmud, Rabbi Simeon ben Gamaliel, the president of the Sanhedrin in the second century CE, held the view that if you did not execute a criminal guilty of a capital offence this encouraged criminal activity. (The Sanhedrin is the name of what used to be the supreme court of the Jewish nation.) Most rabbis, however, did not follow this line. The Mishnah (an earlier commentary on the Torah) tells us that a number of rabbis taught that a Sanhedrin which imposed the death penalty once in seven years could be called bloodthirsty. Rabbi Eleazar ben Azariah felt that it would deserve such a condemnation even if this occurred once in *seventy* years! Rabbis Akiba and Tarphon added: 'Had we been members of the Sanhedrin, no man would ever have been put to death.'

Most rabbis were unhappy with the death penalty and rules were developed which meant that executions were extremely difficult to carry out. There must be two witnesses who will formally warn a person that what he is about to do carries the death penalty, two further witnesses to testify that this warning was given and that the act was then committed.

If, in a vote, all the judges find a person deserving of death, then that person should go free! They felt that if they all agreed, then there was a suspicion of collusion, that is, of fixing the decision beforehand. Finally, the judges themselves had to be involved in the actual execution.

▼   **What do you think might be the effect of insisting that the judges had to be involved in the execution?**

The Holocaust

Although the death penalty is supported by the Torah and the Talmud, and some Jews believe that it should continue, there are many rabbis who believe that it should be abolished. The State of Israel abolished the death penalty in the 1950s but kept it for

RELIGIONS

Yad Vashem – the Holocaust Memorial in Jerusalem for those killed by the Nazis. The thousands of lights are the multi-reflections from only four candles

those found guilty of involvement in the *Holocaust*. This is the word used to describe the events before and during the Second World War when over six million Jews were brutally put to death by the Nazis. There has been one execution for this crime.

▼   **Find out more about the Holocaust. Make some notes on why you think Israel keeps the death penalty for those involved in the Holocaust.**

 Sikhism

The Sikh religion lays great stress on the divine dignity of human beings.

 In every heart there is light:
That light are Thou.
By the light that is of God Himself
Is every soul illumined.

There is no clear instruction on capital punishment in the scriptures. Sikhs, like many other people, have lived mostly in States where the death penalty is part of the legal system.

 Sikhism gives guidance in principles of behaviour and looks to the historical interpretation of the way of life of the Gurus. The Sikh view of capital punishment comes from their view on the use of violence in general. For Sikhs, the resort to arms is only justified under clear conditions. For example, it is permitted to fight against oppression or injustice – and not only injustice towards Sikhs but towards others too. But in the words of the tenth Guru, Guru Gobind Singh, only after all other means of righting the injustice have failed.

It follows from this that killing is justified under certain circumstances. That is, it is justified when fighting in the heat of combat in a situation as already described. But if the enemy surrenders he must not be put to death. He must be allowed to go. Killing in cold blood can never be justified, except possibly of a tyrant intent on continuing to behave in an unjust way.

Executing a prisoner, on the other hand, is without excuse, and would be 'killing in cold blood'. Therefore Sikhs would oppose capital punishment.

During the time of Ranjit Singh – which is the only time Sikhs have formed an independent nation – the death penalty was not used. That is, when Sikhs were able to make laws, capital punishment was not used.

[Indarjit Singh, Editor, *The Sikh Messenger*]

RELIGIONS

▼ General assignments

One thing you are sure to have discovered is that people feel very strongly about the death penalty, both for and against. Perhaps you can think of some reasons why this should be so?

Although most religions seem to allow and sometimes prescribe capital punishment in the documents handed down, many followers today feel that it contradicts the true teaching of their faith.

A petition containing 250,000 signatures calling for the restoration of the death penalty for 'premeditated' murder being presented to the House of Commons in 1972. The Reverend Percy Grey, vice-president of the Citizens Protection Society, is shown carrying one of the parcels of petition signatures. What does 'premeditated' mean? How would you decide whether a murder was premeditated or not?

A demonstration outside Wandsworth Prison, London, on the day of a hanging in 1959. Do you agree with the words on the placard?

▼ **What are the main issues which concern religions in their views about the death penalty?**

Any of the following assignments will help you to reflect on the very important question of capital punishment.

▼ **Make a list of the four words, mentioned in this chapter, which give the main reasons for punishing people. Write one sentence for each explaining what it means.**

▼ **If you think you are against capital punishment, take a position *in favour* of the death penalty and prepare a short speech to show how the four reasons for punishment could be applied to capital punishment.**
Or
If you think you are in favour of capital punishment, take a position *against* the death penalty and prepare a short speech to show how the four reasons for punishment do not justify capital punishment.
Or
Write down your own personal views on the topic, trying to give reasons for where you stand.

▼ **Amnesty International is an organisation which is firmly against the use of the death penalty. Find out more about this organisation and make a report. (You will find the address at the end of this book.)**

▼ **Examine the last report on crime in Britain published by the Home Office, in the reference section of your public library. Make a short summary and comment on whether you think the death penalty has any bearing on this.**

▼ **If it is appropriate, your teacher could help in a class-improvised drama. Take one of the story outlines below and act it out with improvised dialogue. Most important will be the arguments presented concerning the sentence of death.**

a) **In a country where the death penalty is still one of the sentences for murder, a 28-year-old man has been found guilty of murder in the course of a robbery. Invent as much background as you feel necessary and set up a courtroom scene which will begin just before the judge pronounces sentence. In this invented country it is customary for the judge to listen to the views of those present after hearing the final arguments from the prosecuting and defending counsels. Those appointed prosecuting and defending counsels should be given time to prepare their closing statements. The prosecutor will ask for the death penalty. The defender will make a case against. At this point the people present will be asked what further information they require. This may take the form of an interview with the accused or with relatives of the victim or of the accused etc. (Note that this may mean you have to stop the play from time to time in order to agree, for example, who the relatives might be and their probable attitudes.)**

b) Imagine a group of people who have been stranded on a remote island and have been unable to communicate with the rest of the world. They have already set up an organisation with a leader. A young man kills another in the course of an argument about food rations. Some of the group believe that such a crime should be punished by execution otherwise there will be no hope of order being maintained in their community. The leader calls a meeting to take advice from the whole group. Spend a little time agreeing the parts you are going to play and more background details and then act out the meeting. In this case the leader probably should be the teacher. Remember it's not a question of whether the accused did the deed, but *whether* and *how* he should be *punished*. In some cases it is helpful to argue a point of view which you do not hold personally.

▼ If you have been careful to keep the lists referred to on page 141, then now is the time to look at them again and discuss how far your views have changed – if at all.

Twenty-five-year-old James Terry Roach was sent to the electric chair in South Carolina in 1986

▼ Addresses

The following is a selected list of addresses which might be useful to you. Please remember that it takes time to reply to letters and it can be expensive. *All* requests for information should include a stamped addressed envelope.

Check through these rules before you write:

1 Do I need to write? Have I already got access to the information I require?
2 Most of these organisations are run by voluntary helpers and so you should think carefully in advance what you require. Be as specific as possible. Some provide publications lists which you could ask for.
3 Make sure that the same information is not asked by a whole class of students. Ask your teacher to control this.
4 Remember to enclose the necessary return postage. If you are asking for leaflets, this will probably require more than ordinary letter rate.
5 Guarantee payment for any items that are not free of charge.

Buddhism

British Buddhist Association
11 Biddulph Road, London W9 1JA

Buddhist Society
58 Eccleston Square, London SW1V 1PH

Friends of the Western Buddhist Order
London Buddhist Centre, 51 Roman Road
Bethnal Green, London E2 0HU

Indian Buddhist Society of the UK
9 Carlisle Road, Egbaston
Birmingham B16 9BH

Karma Kagya Samye-Ling Tibetan Centre
Eskdalemuir, via Langholm
Dumfries and Galloway OG13 0QL

London Buddhist Vihara
5 Heathfield Gardens, London W4 4JU

London Zen Society
10 Belmont Street, London NW1 8HH

Manjushri Institute
Conishead Priory, Priory Road
Ulverston, Cumbria LA12 9QQ

Shin Buddhist Association of Great Britain
Rev. Jack Austin, 92b Chapmanslade
Westbury, Wiltshire BA13 4AN

Christianity

Catholic Truth Society
40 Eccleston Square, London SW1P 1LT

Christian Medical Fellowship
157 Waterloo Road, London SE1 8XN

Church of England Board for Social Responsibility
Church House, Great Smith Street, London SW1P 3NZ

Church of England Information Office
Church House, Great Smith Street
London SW1P 3NZ

Free Church Federal Council
27 Tavistock Square, London WC1H 9HH

Religious Society of Friends (Quakers)
Friends House, 173 Euston Road, London NW1 2BJ

Salvation Army
101 Queen Victoria Street, London EC4P 4EP

Hinduism

Independent Publishing Company
38 Kennington Lane, London SE11 4LS

ISKCON (International Society for Krishna Consciousness)
10 Soho Street, London W1V 5FA

Ramakrishna Vedanta Centre
Unity House, Blind Lane
Bourne End, Buckinghamshire SL8 5LG

Islam

Islamic Council of Europe
16 Grosvenor Crescent, London SW1 7EP

Islamic Cultural Centre
146 Park Road, London NW8 7RG

Islamic Foundation
223 London Road, Stoneygate,
Leicester LE2 1ZE

Islamic Publications
London Mosque, 16 Gressenhall Road
London SW18 5QL

Muslim Educational Trust
130 Stroud Green Road, London N4 3RZ

Judaism

CJLIC (Central Jewish Lecture and Information Committee)
Board of Deputies of British Jews
Fourth Floor, Woburn House
Upper Woburn Place, London WC1H 0EP

Jewish Education Bureau
8 Westcombe Avenue, Leeds LS8 2BS

Sikhism

Independent Publishing Company
38 Kennington Lane, London SE11 4LS

Sikh Cultural Society of Great Britain
88 Mollison Way, Edgware
Middlesex HA8 5QW

Sikh Missionary Society UK
10 Featherstone Road, Southall
Middlesex UB2 5AA

1 Marriage and Family

Family Planning Association
27 Mortimer Street, London W1N 7RJ

Gingerbread Association for One Parent Families
35 Wellington Street, London WC2E 7BN

Relate, National Marriage Guidance
Herbert Gray College, Little Church Street
Rugby, Warwickshire CV21 3AP

2 Abortion and Medical Ethics

FRAME (Fund for the Replacement of Animals in Medical Experiments)
Eastgate House, 34 Stoney Street
Nottingham NG1 1NB

Health Education Authority
Hamilton House, Mabledon Place
London WC1H 9TX

LIFE Organisation
120 Warwick Street, Royal Leamington Spa
Warwickshire CV32 4QY

National Abortion Campaign
Wesley House, 4 Wild Court
London WC2B 5AU

National Anti-Vivisection Society
51 Harley Street, London W1N 1DD

RSPCA (Royal Society for the Prevention of Cruelty to Animals)
Causeway, Horsham
West Sussex RH12 1HG

Information Officer, St Christopher's Hospice
Lawrie Park Road, London SE26 6DZ

Voluntary Euthanasia Society
13 Prince of Wales Terrace, London W8 5PG

3 The Natural World

Centre for Global Education
University of York, Heslington
Yorkshire YO1 5DD

CWDE (Centre for World Development Education)
Regent's College, Inner Circle
Regent's Park, London NW1 4NS

Council for Environmental Education
School of Education, University of Reading
London Road, Reading
Berkshire RG1 5AQ

Friends of the Earth
26–28 Underwood Street, London N1 7JQ

Greenpeace
30–31 Islington Green, London N1 8BR

WWF UK (World Wide Fund for Nature)
Education Department, Panda House
Weyside Park, Catteshall Lane
Godalming, Surrey GU7 1XR

4 Peace and Conflict

Michael Lyons, Director
British Friends of Neve Shalom
24 Culverlands Close, Green Lane
Stanmore, Middlesex HA7 3AG

CND (Campaign for Nuclear Disarmament)
162 Holloway Road, London N7 8DQ

Centre for Peace Studies
St Martin's College, Lancaster LA1 3JD

Corrymeela Link
PO Box 118, Reading
Berkshire RG1 1SL

FOR (Fellowship of Reconciliation)
40–46 Harleyford Road, London SE11 5AY

Medical Campaign Against Nuclear Weapons
Tress House, 3 Stamford Street
London SE1 9NT

Peace Pledge Union
6 Endsleigh Street, London WC1H 0DX

SANA (Scientists Against Nuclear Arms)
112 Newport Road, New Bradwell
Milton Keynes, Buckinghamshire MK13 0AA

United Nations Association
3 Whitehall Court, London SW1A 2EL

World Disarmament Campaign UK
45–47 Blythe Street, London E2 6LX

5 Capital Punishment

Amnesty International (British Section)
99–119 Rosebery Avenue, London EC1R 4RE

▼ Further Reading

* = teachers' books

Religions

Brown, A., Rankin, J. and Wood, A. *Religions*, Longman, 1988
*Smart, N. and Hecht, R.D. (eds.) *Sacred Texts of the World: A Universal Anthology*, Macmillan, 1982

1 Marriage and Family

Foster, J.L. *Marriage*, Checkpoint 25, Edward Arnold, 1984
McCormack, A.E. *All About Sex*, Teenage Information Series, Chambers, 1987
Mayled, J. *Marriage Customs*, Wayland, 1986

2 Abortion and Medical Ethics

*Atkinson, D. *Life and Death: Moral Choices at the Beginning and End of Life*, OUP, 1986 (*Christian, on euthanasia*)
*Campbell, A.V. and Higgs, R. *In That Case*, Darton, Longman and Todd, 1982 (*for doctors, nurses and social workers*)
Leigh, F. *Man and Animals*, Checkpoint 13, ed. J.L. Foster, Edward Arnold, 1979
*Masri, B.A. *Animals in Islam*, WSPA, 106 Jermyn Street, London SW1Y 6EE
Moran, J. *Medicine*, Checkpoint 34, ed. J.L. Foster, Edward Arnold, 1987
Newson, L. *Animal Rights and Wrongs*, A & C Black, 1990

3 The Natural World

Bright, M. *Pollution and Wildlife*, Franklin Watts, 1987
Bright, M. *Vanishing Habitats*, in *Survival* series, Franklin Watts, 1987
Bunyard, P. and Morgan-Grenville, F. (eds.) *The Green Alternative*, Methuen, 1987
CAFOD/Christian Aid. *Handle with Care*, 1988 (*teachers' resource pack*) CAFOD: Resources, 2 Romero Close, Stockwell Road, London SW9 9TY
Goldsmith, E. and Hildyard, N. (eds.) *The Earth Report*, Mitchell Beazley, 1988
Lyle, S. and Roberts, M. *A Rain Forest Child*, Greenlight Publications, 1988 (*8–13 Pack*)

*Mendes, C. *Fight for the Forest: Chico Mendes in His Own Words*, Latin America Bureau, 1989
*Myers, N. (ed.) *Gaia Atlas of Planet Management: For Today's Caretakers of Tomorrow's World*, Pan, 1985
Palmer, M., Nash, A. and Hattingh, I. (eds.) *Faith and Nature*, Century/WWF, 1988
The New Road, newsletter of the World Wide Fund Network on Conservation and Religion, WWF (*see address list*)
Timberlake, L. *Only One Earth*, BBC Books, 1987

4 Peace and Conflict

Lealman, B. (ed.) *The Nuclear Age*, Christian Education Movement, 1982
Leeds, C.A. *Peace and War: A First Sourcebook*, Stanley Thornes, 1987
*Power, J. *Martin Luther King: A Reassessment*, Peace Pledge Union, n.e. 1988 (*other publications, e.g. on Gandhi, are also available; see address list*)
*Rawding, F.W. *Gandhi*, in *Introduction to the History of Mankind* series, CUP, 1980
*Robertson, E.H. *The Shame of the Sacrifice: Life and Teaching of Dietrich Bonhoeffer*, Hodder & Stoughton, 1987
Weston, S. *Walking Tall*, Bloomsbury, 1989 (*about the Falklands War*)

5 Capital Punishment

Amnesty International (*see address list*) publishes a number of books, reports, videos and education packs
Church of England Board for Social Responsibility. *Capital Punishment*, 1984 (*see address list*)
*Glover, J. *Causing Death and Saving Lives*, Penguin, 1977

▼ Index

▼ Acknowledgements

We are grateful to the following for permission to reproduce copyright material:

Bible Society for an adapted extract from *The Good News Bible* © Bible Societies/Collins; Carol C Kimball, the Executor of the Estate of E A Burtt, for his translation of an extract by Sutta Nipata in *The Teachings of the Compassionate Buddha* edited, with commentary by E A Burtt (Pub. The New American Library), copyright © 1955 by Edwin A Burtt; Cambridge University Press for an abridged extract from *Practical Ethics* (1979) by Peter Singer; Cambridge University Press for extracts from *New English Bible* © 1970 by Oxford and Cambridge University Presses; The Central Board of Finance of the Church of England for extracts from *The Alternative Service Book 1980* (Pub. Hodder & Stoughton), copyright © The Central Board of Fin-ance of the Church of England; Central Television Enterprises Ltd for an abridged extract from the television programme *The Green Revolution* March 1990, produced by Goldhawk Film and Television Productions Ltd/Central Television Enterprises Ltd; Christian Medical Fellowship for a poem from *The Dying Patient* by Dr R G Twycross; the author's agent for an abridged extract from *Whose Life Is It Anyway?* by Brian Clark (Pub. Amber Lane Press 1978); Curzon Press Ltd for extracts from *A Manual of Hadith* (1988) by Maulana Muhammad Ali; Darton, Longman & Todd Ltd for extracts from *Catholic Prayer Book* edited by Allen Bullen, copyright © 1970 by Darton, Longman & Todd Ltd; Guru Nanak Foundation U.K. for extracts from *The Japji* (The Sikh Morning Prayer), Publication No. 5, translation by S Khushwant Singh; Macmillan Accounts and Administration for adapted extracts from *Sacred Texts of the World* by Smart and Hecht; Mariapolis Ltd for their translation of an abridged extract from article by Takae Ishii in *New City* December 1986; The National Council of the Churches of Christ in the USA for scripture quotations from the *Revised Standard Version Common Bible* (Pub. Collins), copyright © 1973 by the Division of Christian Education of the National Council of the Churches of Christ in the USA; The Open University for an extract from *Selection of Hymns of Guru Nanak from Adi Granth* (1978) trans. D A Thomas; the author's agent and The estate of the late Sonia Brownell Orwell for an extract from *Collected Essays* by George Orwell (Pub. Secker & Warburg); Quartet Books Ltd for an abridged extract from *Abortion: The Whole Story* by Mary Kenny (1986); Random Century Group on behalf of Friends of the Earth for an extract from the foreword by Jonathan Porritt from *How To Be Green* by John Button (Pub. Century Hutchinson 1989); Reform Synagogues of Great Britain for an extract from *Forms of Prayer Vol. 1, Daily & Sabbath Prayerbook*, 1977; The Sikh Cultural Society of Great Britain for an abridged extract from *The Sikh Marriage Ceremony* (Publication No 7) and extract from *An Introduction to Sikh Belief* (Publication No 2); The Society for Promoting Christian Knowledge for an abridged extract from *Christianity and the Rights of Animals* by A Linzey; the author, Jacqueline A Southee of FRAME, for her quotation in Richard Girling's article in the *Sunday Times Magazine* 12.11.89; Times Newspapers Ltd for extracts from articles by Clifford Longley in *The Times* 17.8.76. and Aileen Ballantyne in *The Sunday Times* 4.3.90. © Times Newspapers Ltd 1976, 1990; Unwin Hyman Ltd for extracts from *The Koran Interpreted* by A J Arberry; World Wide Fund for Nature for extracts of declarations on religion and nature made at World Wide Fund's 25th anniversary celebrations in Assisi, Italy in September 1986; the author, Inayatullah Zaigham, for extracts from his letter in *The Independent* 29.7.89.

Additional sources

The Independent on Sunday 4.2.90, p.19; Ven Dr H Saddhatissa & R Webb *A Buddhist's Manual*, p. 25; J Prickett (ed.) *Marriage and the Family*, pp. 25, 30; Pastoral Constitution on the Church in the Modern World (Vatican II), pp. 28, 68; J-P Bagot *How to Understand Marriage*, p. 29; IPPF: *Islam and Family Planning*, pp. 33, 34, 35, 73; Z Khan *Islam and Human Rights*, pp. 33, 73; S Strassfeld *Second Jewish Catalog*, pp. 39, 74; *Encyclopaedia Judaica*, vol. 6, p. 39; SPUC: *SPUC Speaks to Christians*, p. 52; M Kenny *Abortion: The Whole Story*, p. 54; D McDonald *Ethical Issues in Reproductive Medicine*, p. 54; T Vernay *The Secret Life of the Unborn Child*, p. 54; N Scarisbrick, J Richardson in *Women's Own* magazine, June 1983, p. 54; M Palmer, A Nash & I Hattingh (eds) *Faith and Nature*, pp. 67, 90, 98, 100; W Purcell *Euthanasia*, pp. 68-9; K Brown (ed.) *The Essential Teachings of Hinduism*, pp. 70, 72, 77, 128; M Palmer *Worlds of Difference*, p. 72; L Timberlake *Only One Earth*, p. 84; S Weston *Walking Tall*, p. 108; Yorkshire TV video: *The Falklands War: The Untold Story*, pp. 108, 109, 110; M Arthur *Above All Courage*, pp. 110-11; RMEP: *No Compromise: Faith in Action* series, p. 118; Peace Education Project: *Conscientious Objectors: Pacifism*, p. 121 and *Conscientious Objectors: 1916 to the Present Day*, p. 121; R Runcie & B Hume (eds) *Prayers for Peace*, pp. 124, 125, 132, 137; C Humphries (ed.) *The Wisdom of the Buddha*, pp. 124, 125; Peace Education Project: *Gandhi: A short introduction*, p. 131; K Brown & M Palmer *The Essential Teachings of Islam*, pp. 132, 133; D Shapiro *The Jewish Attitude towards War and Peace* in L Jung (ed.) *Israel of Tomorrow*, p. 135; Manchester University Press: *Textual Sources for the Study of Sikhism*, p. 136; *New City*, pp. 138-9; B Bhutto *Daughter of the East*, p. 142; Allen & Unwin: *The Sacred Writings of the Sikhs*, p. 164.

▼ Acknowledgements

We are grateful to the following for permission to reproduce photographs and other copyright material:

Andes Press Agency (Carlos Reyes), pages 69, 125; Mohamed Ansar, page 93; Robin Bath, page 24; from: *The Earth Report*, Mitchell Beazley, pages 81, 86; Bettmann Newsphotos (UPI), page 143; W. Braun, page 163; Private Collection/Bridgeman Art Library, page 155; Channel Four Television, page 16; *Daily Mirror*, 22.9.89, page 53 (John Frost); © DACS 1991, page 91 (Bridgeman Art Library); Mark Edwards, page 19; E. T. Archive, page 156; Mary Evans Picture Library, pages 140, 151; Chris Fairclough Colour Library, pages 12, 27; Sally & Richard Greenhill, pages 9, 15, 33, 55; Greenpeace Communications Ltd, page 104–5; Hutchison Library, pages 31 (Nancy Durrell McKenna), 82 (J. Von Puttkamer); Mauritshius, The Hague/Bridgeman Art Library, page 75; Tony Morrison, South American Pictures, page 83; The National Gallery, London/Bridgeman Art Library, page 126; Neve Shalom/Wahat al-Salam, pages 138, 139; Christine Osborne Pictures, page 103; Peace Pledge Union, page 116; © Ann & Bury Peerless Slide Resources & Picture Library; pages 40, 71, 129, 130, 136; Popperfoto, pages 109 (UPI), 123 (Reuter); Rex Features, pages 112, 167 (Colombia Newspapers/Sipa Press); Peter Sanders, pages 99, 133; Science Photo Library, pages 47 *above left* (Petit Format/Nestlé), 47 *above right* (James Stevenson), 47 *below* (David Leah), 51 (Hank Morgan), 58 (Martin Dohrn/IVF Unit, Cromwell Hospital), 79 (Earth Satellite Corporation), 89 (Ken Biggs); Select Photos, page 153 (Dario Mitidieri); Frank Spooner Pictures, pages 49 (Gamma), 111 (François Lochon/Gamma), 115 (K. Kurita); Sygma, page 87 (Regis Bossu); Syndication International, pages 57, 61, 165; Tantra Designs, page 98; Topham Picture Source, pages 117, 119, 159 (Associated Press); from *Conscientious Objectors, 1916 to the present day*, Tressell Publications, 1988, page 120; Tropix, page 11 (V.J. Birley); WWF, page 94 (Hans J. Burkard); Zefa Picture Library, pages 37, 134 (W. Braun).

Cover photos: Young black woman kissing child, Sally & Richard Greenhill; Friends of the Earth demonstration: *Stop Acid Rain*, Network (photo: Goldwater); Air pollution from coal plant chimneys, Tony Stone (photo: David Higgs).

Longman Group UK Limited
Longman House, Burnt Mill, Harlow,
Essex CM20 2JE, England
and Associated Companies throughout the world

© Longman Group Limited 1991

First published 1991
Second impression 1992

ISBN 0 582 03307 1

Set in 10/14pt Helvetica Light
Printed in Hong Kong
SWT/02